LESSON PLANS & TEACHER'S MANUAL
BUILDING THINKING SKILLS®
Book 3 – Figural

SERIES TITLES
BUILDING THINKING SKILLS®—PRIMARY
BUILDING THINKING SKILLS®—BOOK 1
BUILDING THINKING SKILLS®—BOOK 2
BUILDING THINKING SKILLS®—BOOK 3 FIGURAL
BUILDING THINKING SKILLS®—BOOK 3 VERBAL

SANDRA PARKS AND HOWARD BLACK

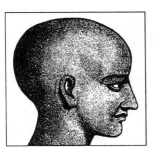

© 1987
CRITICAL THINKING PRESS & SOFTWARE
(formerly Midwest Publications)
P.O. Box 448 • Pacific Grove • CA 93950-0448
Phone 800-458-4849 • FAX 408-393-3277
ISBN 0-89455-322-4
Printed in the United States of America

TABLE OF CONTENTS

3

ACKNOWLEDGMENTS

The developers of this program wish to acknowledge the contribution of many people with whom they have worked over the years—teachers, students, and parents.

Gary Rito of the Dade County Public Schools contributed many valuable comments and suggestions as we developed these lessons.

Carole Bannes, Senior Editor for Midwest Publications, suggested many of the Curriculum Applications, as well as contributing careful editing, formatting, and computer graphics.

Howard and Sandra Black

INTRODUCTION

ALTERNATIVES FOR USE

The *Building Thinking Skills* books may be used in conjunction with content objectives or as a separate course of study. The decision regarding whether to use thinking skills instruction as a supplement to the existing curriculum objectives, or as a separate course, depends on several factors: (1) how thinking skills instruction can be scheduled in the existing school program; (2) how thinking skills instruction can be most easily managed and evaluated; (3) how much curriculum and staff development time can be committed to the program; (4) whether teachers are more receptive to an additional curriculum or a strategy for existing instructional objectives; (5) the extent to which student proficiency at thinking skills is expected to improve performance in content objectives.

Research in cognitive skills instruction indicates that if content objectives in cognitive skills are taught in the same lesson, the thinking process is likely to be less emphasized than the content objectives. Since teachers and students are held accountable for content information, related cognitive processes are seldom identified or developed. Often, content objectives employ cognitive skills, at which students may be less proficient than expected. Content objectives may presume to be teaching thinking skills when, actually, a lesson is an application of, and not instruction in, the skill that is being addressed.

Content objectives may prescribe a cognitive task, such as classification, without realizing the subtle steps that are involved in the ability to classify. As a result, the teacher has not taught classification, the learner has not perceived that he or she has learned it, and neither understand why the lesson is not effective. Integrating thinking skills totally into content objectives may seem appealing from a curriculum development standpoint, but may be superficial in implementation. Thinking skills instruction totally "hidden" in the content curriculum is difficult to document and evaluate.

Thinking skills instruction as a separate course of study offers an alternative curriculum design. In an independent structured program, teachers know that they are teaching, and students know that they are learning, the cognitive skills required in the academic curriculum. Focusing on teaching a skill encourages adequate explanation and practice. Students recognize their growing competence in the kinds of tasks required in schooling. A structured program is relatively easy to observe and evaluate.

Cognitive skill learning should be tied to applications at school or at home, if the learner is to perceive that this instruction is relevant or helpful. Students may not attend conscientiously to a "game" or make the expected connections in academic objectives. The teaching of cognitive skills may be fairly superficial without the reinforcement of use. When thinking skills instruction is perceived as a "separate curriculum," it becomes vulnerable to changes in priorities within the school and may be easily eliminated as a "fad." Teachers tend to resist instruction that they do not perceive as relevant to the objectives for which they are already held accountable.

The authors recommend that thinking skills activities be implemented as a structured sequential course of study, offered in conjunction with content objectives. Because content objectives usually apply, rather than develop, thinking skills, the thinking skill instruction should be offered just prior to the corresponding content objective. In this option, the thinking skills course is spread out within the existing school program. Hence, one can be assured of offering an identifiable, structured program as a method of teaching content objectives. The linkage between thinking skills instruction and school performance is accomplished by identifying these skills in the existing school program. The editorial process produces a cognitive skills curriculum tailored to district needs, rather than implementation of a "packed program." This articulated program allows supervisors to identify and evaluate instruction, but is accepted by teachers, because thinking skills instruction makes their existing instruction more effective.

PROGRAM DESIGN

Selection and organization of skills. The cognitive skills developed in this series were selected because of their significance in the academic disciplines. These four skills (similarities and differences, sequences, classifications, and analogies) are required in all content areas, including the arts. Since improved school performance is an important goal of thinking skills instruction, many variations of the skills are presented.

Four cognitive skills are offered in the same order that the child develops intellectually. Distinguishing similarities and differences is integral to the learner's ability to put things in order, to group items by class, and to think analogously. Skills are presented in figural and verbal form, following the developmental process of conceptualization in concrete, figural form before the development of abstract, verbal reasoning. The organization of the book includes:

Figural Similarities
Figural Sequences
Figural Classifications
Figural Analogies

Comparable skills in verbal form are presented in *Building Thinking Skills 3—Verbal:*

Verbal Similarities (Synonyms & Antonyms)
Verbal Sequences
Verbal Classifications
Verbal Analogies

The teacher may select either the figural or the verbal strand as a sequence of instruction, may alternate between the two forms, or may schedule the thinking skills exercises as they occur in content objectives. In any case, similarities-and-differences exercises should be offered early in the course of instruction since that skill is basic to more complex ones.

Item design. In each strand, exercises have been designed in the manner that the developing child learns: cognition, evaluation, and convergent production. The simplest form of a task is recognizing the correct answer among several choices. These cognition items have the directions: "select." Next in difficulty is the ability to explain or rank items. This evaluation step clarifies for the learner the relationships between objects or concepts. The evaluation items contain the direction: "rank" or "explain."

When the learner must supply a single, correct answer from his own background and memory, the task becomes more difficult. This convergent production step is designated by the heading: "supply." Teachers may find that it becomes helpful to explain concepts in any discipline if they remember the simple "select, explain, then supply" process. Teachers familiar with J. P. Guilford's *Structure of Intellect* model will recognize the cognition, evaluation, and convergent production factors in both figural and verbal form in these exercises.

INSTRUCTIONAL METHODS

Piagetian learning theory indicates that the learner proceeds from the concrete, manipulative form of tasks to the semi-concrete, paper-and-pencil form of the task, and finally to the abstract, verbal form. The *Building Thinking Skills* series is based on that progression. Ideally, students should practice each cognitive task in manipulative form. Manipulatives, such as attribute blocks and tangrams, are commonly available or easily made from inexpensive materials.

The student book is the paper-and-pencil form of exercise. Class discussion maximizes student benefit from the paper-and-pencil exercises.

The third step in this process—abstract, verbal expression of the task—is involved in the class discussion of the exercises. This important step reinforces and confirms the thinking processes the learner used to carry out the task. While there are many subtleties in thinking that we cannot express, the skills in this program are relatively common ones and can be discussed relatively easily. The discussion process clarifies what the learner did to get the answer, and differentiates that process from similar ones.

Discussion allows learners to see alternative processing strategies. This technique allows students to understand other ways of getting an answer. For the gifted students, discussion provides insight regarding how other equally bright learners can arrive at correct answers by different analysis. Hence, discussion demonstrates differences in learning styles, a strategy that allows students to recognize and value other people's processes for solving problems.

Discussion reinforces the learner's memory of the thinking process, increasing transfer to similar tasks in the content areas. When the student recognizes that he or she has correctly thought through this kind of task in a nonthreatening learning situation, the learner's confidence in his or her ability to solve similar problems in a different context is enhanced.

Class discussion also provides verbal stimulation for figural learners. This strategy is helpful for the student whose language skills are underdeveloped. Emphasizing the deficit, rather than taking advantage of cognitive strength, leads to frustration and low self-esteem for the learner. Figural proficiency is common in students whose background or hearing impairment has resulted in limited language acquisition. Since the intellectual development of the learner continues in a limited way in spite of the lack of language stimulation, figural and intuitive tasks are likely to be cognitive strengths of such students. Implementation of similar Midwest Publications' figural materials with minority students, learning disabled, or hearing impaired students, has indicated that "giving words" to a figural task can be an effective strategy in language acquisition. Since most academic learning is in verbal form, this linkage becomes particularly important.

Figural exercises offer figural stimulation for verbal learners. These students are often academically achieving learners whose ability to verbalize may mask limited conceptualization skills. This is the case, for example, when students memorize the patterns of words appropriate for solving various types of mathematical problems. The teacher and the learner may both assume that the learner visualizes and conceptualizes a process when, in fact, such learning may be superficial memorization. When the learner forgets the formula or algorithm, he or she has no basis for learning how to do the problem. The verbal learner may use his or her verbal skills to reinforce and clarify figural perceptions until such time as he or she becomes skillful enough to perceive relationships without verbal analysis of the task.

Figural observation skills are necessary for scientific observation. Lack of figural skills may explain why a student who can take a textbook test quite well may perform less satisfactorily in a laboratory exercise.

Discussion Principles. Discussion is the process by which the learner clarifies subtle aspects of processing the exercises. This clarification distinguishes a task from similar ones and provides alternative and creative ways of getting an answer. Through discussion, the learner ties a task to others in his or her experience and anticipates situations in which that skill is helpful. For effective explanation and transfer of the skill, the explanation should always be **FROM EXPERIENCE TO EXPERIENCE.**

In introducing a skill, the teacher should identify a real-word or academic experience in which the learner has used that skill. This reference cues the learner that this task is one with which the learner already has some experience and competence. It signals the learner that the task is useful and reduces anxiety about being able to master it.

After explanation and guided practice, the learner should be asked to tie this skill to another use in his or her experience. This memory aid increases the learner's confidence in reasoning and encourages transfer of the skill.

For learners who have not been successful in school, the relevance and perceived usefulness of thinking skills may be a factor in how thoroughly the learner will attend to the task. While improved thinking skills may improve school performance, low-functioning students seldom expect that effect and require some extrinsic motive for attempting the exercise.

Because an important goal of thinking skills instruction is improved school performance, both teachers and students should become aware of the applications of thinking skills in the content curriculum. This application reinforces newly mastered skills, improves student confidence, and facilitates new content learning. The focus of thinking skills instruction is improving teaching and learning. That goal is best realized by frequent identification of these four thinking skills whenever teachers and students encounter similar tasks. Thinking skills instruction is a method for improving content learning, as well as a new element of the curriculum.

RATIONALE AND DESCRIPTION OF SKILLS

FIGURAL SIMILARITIES

The FIGURAL SIMILARITIES strand features activities to develop visual discrimination skills and to improve students' perceptions of congruence and similarity.

Visual discrimination in its simplest forms involves geometric shapes and the appearance of letters. At more complex levels, visual discrimination is required in scientific classification. In elementary school mathematics programs, the concepts of congruence and similarity are utilized in establishing geometric definitions and developing perceptions of area and volume.

The ability to discern similarities and differences is necessary before the learner can place objects in order, classify them, or make analogous comparisons.

In the FIGURAL SIMILARITIES strand, students exercise cognition in selecting the correct shape among subtly different ones. The learner evaluates whether or not a shape matches others, or whether a shape appears in a more complex design. Types of exercises in this strand include:

1. Shape analysis and matching
2. Finding and combining shapes
3. Evaluating and producing equal shapes
4. Recognition of shapes necessary to complete a whole figure
5. Reducing or enlarging shapes
6. Symmetry
7. Volume perception

Difficulty in processing these items will probably affect the other figural tasks as well. If individual students have unusual difficulty processing the items, the teacher can administer the *Structure of Intellect* (SOI) *Learning Abilities Test* or the vision form of the *SOI Learning Abilities Test* to assess students' visual perception skills. More extensive practice of figural skills may be obtained from Midwest Publications' *Figural Similarities* series or from the *Structure of Intellect Sourcebook.* For information on SOI materials and services, contact SOI Institute, 343 Richmond St., El Segundo, CA 90245.

FIGURAL SEQUENCES

The FIGURAL SEQUENCES strand provides exercises that develop visual discrimination and that promote sequential reasoning. Identifying sequences in figural form sharpens observational skills and promotes students' reasoning ability regardless of language development.

Visual discrimination activities may be helpful in promoting word decoding for upper elementary students having reading difficulty. Reading development requires the learner to recognize subtle differences in the shapes and sequences of letters or the appearance of a whole word. FIGURAL SEQUENCES employs visual discrimination in a form unrelated to students' previous unsuccessful experiences with written passages.

Visual discrimination skills are fundamental to elementary science and mathematics instruction. Relational observations of rotation, reflection, size change, and shape change are basic observations in geometry, botany, zoology, and geology.

Figural reasoning instruction allows primary gifted students or mature, low-reading-level students to carry out complex analysis and evaluation tasks. Since the culture-free form of this material does not require a standard English, vocabulary or well-developed reading skills, these exercises can be used with non-English-speaking students.

In the FIGURAL SEQUENCES strand, students are introduced to a variety of skills in sequencing: adding or subtracting detail in figures; changing size, shape, or color of figures in a sequence; rotation and reflection of shapes; and rearrangement of figures in a sequence. Types of exercises in this strand include:

1. Recognizing the next figure in a sequence
2. Producing the next figure in a sequence
3. Recognizing rotation and reflection of plane and solid figures
4. Paper folding
5. Pattern folding

More extensive practice of figural sequencing skills can be obtained in Midwest Publications' booklets: *Figural Sequences A-1, B-1,* and *C-1*.

FIGURAL CLASSIFICATION

FIGURAL CLASSIFICATION exercises develop the ability to group or organize objects by similar characteristics. Classification is a significant concept-building process that builds skills primarily associated with the science curriculum. However, classification is a helpful study skill, promoting visual discrimination, memory, observation, organizing skills, and practical problem-solving ability.

The student uses classification as an observational tool. By expecting to find similar or different characteristics, the learner examines and understands new material. Classification is a tool in the learner's ability to assimilate new information and to accommodate his or her old categories to include new experiences.

Classification assists the student in visualizing relationships and provides a practical problem-solving technique. Venn diagrams and matrices are useful to show that items have some or all variables in common, a graphic device for showing relationships quickly and easily to other people. These simple logic techniques are integral to computer logic and set theory.

The FIGURAL CLASSIFICATION exercises increase sequentially in complexity and proceed through the learning sequence:

1. Classifying by shape
2. Classifying by pattern
3. Classifying by shape and pattern
4. Describing characteristics of a class
5. Matching classes
6. Completing or forming a class
7. Producing another member of a class
8. Using diagrams to depict overlapping classes

For diagnosis of students' figural classification skills, use the *Structure of Intellect* (SOI) *Learning Abilities Test.* More extensive practice of figural classification skills may be obtained from Midwest Publications' *Figural Classification* series or the *Structure of Intellect Sourcebook.* For information on SOI materials and services, contact SOI Institute, 343 Richmond St., El Segundo, CA 90245.

FIGURAL ANALOGIES

The FIGURAL ANALOGIES strand provides exercises that develop visual discrimination skills and that promote inductive reasoning. Teaching students to identify analogous relationships in figural form sharpens observational skills and promotes students' reasoning ability. Analogous relationships are basic to all fields of study. Analogies are expressed as imagery in literature, ratios in mathematics, and as analysis techniques in geometry, natural, and social sciences. While teachers use analogies in explaining concepts, students seldom practice this useful relational technique before they encounter analogies on objective tests.

In the FIGURAL ANALOGIES strand, students are introduced to analogous relationships A : B :: C : D. Students analyze the components, recognize the relationships, and complete analogies by selecting and drawing the missing figure. The exercises in this strand are not graded and require little reading skill. Types of figural analogies include:

1. Color or size change
2. Rotations and reflections
3. Change in detail

RECOMMENDED TESTS FOR EVALUATING THE EFFECTIVENESS OF THE *BUILDING THINKING SKILLS®* SERIES

1. Any standardized content test currently utilized by your district will reflect increases in students' academic performance that result from better thinking skills and can be used to measure the effectiveness of the *Building Thinking Skills®* series.

2. Tests are also available to measure growth in cognitive skills specifically. These tests include the following:

   - **Cognitive Abilities Test**
     Riverside Publishing Company
     8420 Bryn Mawr Ave.
     Chicago, IL 60631
     800-323-9540 • 312-693-0325 (fax)

   - **Developing Cognitive Abilities Test**
     American College Testronics (formerly American Testronics)
     P.O. Box 2270
     Iowa City, IA 52244
     800-553-0030 • 319-337-1578 (fax)

   - **Test of Cognitive Skills**
     CTB-McGraw Hill
     P.O. Box 150
     Monterey, CA 93942-0150
     800-538-9547 • 800-282-0266 (fax)

   - **Structure of Intellect Learning Abilities Test**
     S.O.I. Institute
     P.O. Box D
     Vida, OR 97488
     503-896-3936 • 503-896-3983 (fax)

   - **Differential Aptitude Tests**
     Psychological Corporation
     Order Service Center
     P.O. Box 839954
     San Antonio, TX 78283-3954
     800-228-0752 • 800-232-1223 (fax)

   - **WISC-III**
     Psychological Corporation
     Order Service Center
     P.O. Box 839954
     San Antonio, TX 78283-3954
     800-228-0752 • 800-232-1223 (fax)

GUIDE TO USING THE LESSON PLANS

HEADING: Corresponds to the subhead at the top of each student workbook page.

STRAND: Identifies which of the eight skills is being developed.

ADDITIONAL MATERIALS: Lists necessary materials and supplies needed for demonstrating the lesson, e.g., transparencies, models, marking pens.

INTRODUCTION: Indicates to the student where he or she has seen or used a similar kind of learning. *Throughout the Lesson Plans, sample teacher statements appear in bold italic type.*

OBJECTIVE: Explains to the student what he or she can expect to learn in the lesson.

DEMONSTRATION/EXPLANATION: Offers a concrete form of the task, and/or illustrates by modeling, procedures which students can duplicate. Students may also prepare models or materials similar to those suggested. Facilitators conducting a lesson should verbalize their own thinking process. This modeling provides cues to students for thinking through the task. Procedures for conducting the lessons are printed in standard type.

GUIDED PRACTICE: Controlled practice allows the teacher to identify answer or processing errors. To check for understanding, **GUIDED PRACTICE** should be followed by **class discussion.** Answers and explanation to exercises are included.

INDEPENDENT PRACTICE: Practice exercises for promoting skill mastery.

DISCUSSION TIPS: After students have had the opportunity to complete the exercises independently, the teacher debriefs the class by discussion of the exercises. Significant terms and concepts are stressed at this point. Discussion should include student explanations for rejection of incorrect answers, as well as confirmation of correct ones. This process promotes clarification of subtle perceptions in the thinking skill lessons.

ANSWERS: Provides answers and explanations for **INDEPENDENT PRACTICE** exercises.

FOLLOW-UP REFERENT: Ties the skill back to the experience of the student, completing the "from experience back to experience" loop, and cues the student regarding possible future uses of that skill.

CURRICULUM APPLICATION: Indicate possible content objectives which feature the skill or require it as a prerequisite. The curriculum linkage examples are not intended to be complete, but rather to provide ideas for using that skill.

EXTENDING ACTIVITIES: Suggests more complex forms of the task.

BUILDING THINKING SKILLS™
LESSON PLANS for BOOK 3–FIGURAL

FIGURAL SIMILARITIES AND DIFFERENCES

MATCHING FIGURES

STRAND: Figural Similarities   **PAGES:** 1–2

ADDITIONAL MATERIALS:
Transparency of Transparency Master (TM) #1 (cut apart as indicated)
Washable transparency marker

INTRODUCTION:
When you were very little, you learned to pick out things that were similar to each other. You could find a ball, regardless of the color or size, because you knew what "a ball" looked like. If you have ever helped set a table or build something in a workshop, you have probably been asked, "Please bring me one just like this."

OBJECTIVE:
In these exercises you will compare four figures to find which two are exactly alike.

DEMONSTRATION/EXPLANATION:
Project the top section of TM #1 (**EXAMPLE**, student workbook page 1).
You are to look for figures which are exactly alike. Small details in line, angle, or pattern determine the difference. Look for key features. Are the outside shapes of these figures the same?
Indicate the four shapes. Answer: Yes. Confirm answers by overlaying movable figure **1** on each figure.
How many lines does each figure have in its pattern?
Answer: Three; one vertical and two diagonal.
Look at the right side of each figure. The point where the diagonal line intersects the right side is a key feature. The diagonal line appears to intersect this vertical at the same point in Figures b and d, at a lower point in Figure a, and at a higher point in Figure c.
Use movable figure **2** to overlay each of the four figures.
This figure does not match Figures a or c...
Demonstrate.
...but does match Figures b and d.
Circle Figures **b** and **c** on the transparency.
Circle the matching figures in each of the following exercises.

GUIDED PRACTICE:
EXERCISES: **A-1, A-2, A-3**
Give students sufficient time to complete these exercises. Then, using the demonstration

methodology above, have them discuss and explain their choices and give reasons for eliminating the unchosen answers.
ANSWERS: **A-1** a and c;   **A-2** b and c;   **A-3** a and d

INDEPENDENT PRACTICE:
Assign exercises **A-4** through **A-7**

DISCUSSION TIPS:
Students need to know the terms **square**, **circle**, **rectangle**, **parallelogram**, **triangle**, **right triangle**, and **trapezoid**. During discussion, encourage them to describe the shapes as accurately as possible, e.g., **pointed**, **shorter**, **taller**, **wider**, etc. Be sure to emphasize the importance of direction. The shapes *must* face in the same direction.

ANSWERS:
A-4 a and d;   **A-5** a and c;   **A-6** a and c;   **A-7** a and b

FOLLOW-UP REFERENT:
   When might you need to identify matching shapes or figures?
Examples: matching model parts; recognizing differences in shapes of leaves, insects, road signs, makes of cars

CURRICULUM APPLICATION:
Language Arts: visual discrimination for reading readiness
Mathematics: figural similarity and congruence in geometry
Science: observing differences in cell shapes or tissue patterns through a microscope; electrical circuit diagrams
Social Studies: matching puzzle sections to geographic features; using legends to locate map features, e.g., parks, airports, rest or camping areas
Enrichment Areas: recognizing road signs by shape; discerning patterns in art, written music, or dance steps; identifying airplanes, ships, and other transports by shape

EXTENDING ACTIVITIES:
Area Perception, Book A-1, pp. 43–54
Figural Similarities, Book D-1, pp. 2–4

WHICH FIGURE DOES NOT MATCH?

STRAND: Figural Similarities   **PAGES:** 3–5

ADDITIONAL MATERIALS:
Transparency of TM #2 (cut apart as indicated)
Attribute blocks (optional)
Washable transparency marker

INTRODUCTION:

"One of these things is not like the others. One of these things just doesn't belong."
You probably heard that rhyme on <u>Sesame Street</u> *when you were much younger.*
That basic idea is used every time you look for something that appears different
from the others around it.

OBJECTIVE:

In these exercises you will find one figure that is different from the others.

DEMONSTRATION/EXPLANATION:

Project TM #2.

As in the previous exercises, you are to look for key features. Examine the outside
shapes and each inside angle and line. Do each of these figures have the same
shape and size?

Answer: Yes.

Does each face the same direction?

Answer: Yes.

Now examine the pattern. How many lines does each figure have in its pattern?

Answer: Three.

Are the three lines exactly the same in each of the figures?

Answer: No.

Which one is different and how is it different?

Answer: The diagonal line in Figure **b** is the opposite direction. Use the movable figure to
overlay each figure as you confirm this answer.

The movable figure matches Figure a exactly; all the lines are the same.

Lay the movable figure on Figure **b.**

The movable figure does not match Figure b. The diagonal line is the opposite
direction.

Mark Figure **b** with an X, then overlay Figure **c.**

The movable figure matches Figure c exactly.

Overlay the movable figure on Figure **d.**

The movable figure matches Figure d exactly. Since only Figure b does not match,
only that figure is to be crossed out.

GUIDED PRACTICE:

EXERCISES: **A-8, A-9**

Give students sufficient time to complete these exercises. Then, using the demonstration
methodology above, have them discuss and explain their choices.

ANSWERS: **A-8** b;   **A-9** b

INDEPENDENT PRACTICE:

Assign exercises **A-10** through **A-21**

DISCUSSION TIPS:

Remind students of the words used in the previous lesson to identify shapes and sizes.
Words emphasized in this lesson should include: **square, circle, rectangle, pentagon,
parallelogram, triangle, right triangle, slanted, pointed,** and **narrow.** The difference in this

exercise is the emphasis on the word *NOT*. Students may wish to color in key features with markers to confirm perception of subtle patterns.

ANSWERS:
A-10 a; **A-11** c; **A-12** c; **A-13** e; **A-14** a; **A-15** b; **A-16** e; **A-17** c; **A-18** b; **A-19** c; **A-20** e; **A-21** d

FOLLOW-UP REFERENT:
> *When might you be asked to identify something shaped or patterned differently from others in a group?*

Examples: utensils, hardware, or tools improperly stored; distinguishing among different makes of cars, engines, or motors; finding errors or exceptions in needlework patterns

CURRICULUM APPLICATION:
Language Arts: visual discrimination exercises; distinguishing among formats for business letters or memos; identifying consistency errors in layouts of school yearbooks, magazines, or newspapers
Mathematics: similarity and congruence exercises in geometry
Science: observations or activities involving shape or appearance of leaves, insects, animals, or rocks
Social Studies: distinguishing among land forms according to size and shape; recognizing graphic variations in charts or graphs
Enrichment Areas: distinguishing among purposes of road signs by shape; distinguishing among note or rest values in music

EXTENDING ACTIVITIES:
Brain Stretchers, Book 1, pp. 1–3

FINDING AND TRACING PATTERNS

STRAND: Figural Similarities   **PAGES:** 6–10

ADDITIONAL MATERIALS:
Transparency of student workbook page 6 (cut apart as indicated below)
Washable transparency marker
Crayons or markers (optional)

INTRODUCTION:
> *In previous exercises you identified figures that were the same and figures that were different. Some figures differed only in a very small detail, and you had to examine each line and angle in the pattern to find the correct answers.*

OBJECTIVE:
> *In these exercises you will find and trace a pattern hidden in a larger design. The pattern must face in the same direction in the complex design, but it may have extra lines.*

DEMONSTRATION/EXPLANATION:
Cut out the pattern piece and answer choices in the **EXAMPLE** from the transparency of page 6, removing the circle from **b**. Place all pieces on the overhead projector. Relocate the pattern piece to show it can be moved around.

>*Any time you move the pattern you must keep it facing in the same direction. Do not turn the pattern as you move it, just slide it. This is the pattern you will look for in each figure. Every shape, outline, inside line, and angle must match exactly.*

Point to figure **a**, indicating each section as you explain.

>*The horizontal and vertical lines in the pattern seem to be in the same places in this figure.*

Place the pattern over figure **a** and trace the horizontal and vertical lines over the matching parts. If possible, use a colored transparency marker to make the pattern more visible. Move the pattern off of figure **a**.

>*Now look at the diagonal lines. How many diagonals are in the pattern?*

Answer: Four; two that intersect within the shape and one in each of the bottom corners.

>*Are there four diagonals in figure **a**?*

Answer: Yes.

>*Are they the same as the diagonals in the pattern?*

Answer: No.

>*How are they different?*

Possible answers: The intersecting diagonals meet at a higher point in figure **a** than in the pattern; the corner diagonals are shorter; figure **a** has two pairs of parallel diagonals, those in the pattern are not parallel. Place the pattern piece over figure **a**.

>*You can see that none of the diagonal lines match, so the pattern does not fit figure **a**.*

Point to figure **b**.

>*Is the pattern hidden in figure **b**?*

Answer: Yes. Trace the pattern in figure **b** with the transparency marker, then lay the pattern over the figure.

>*All of the edges fit exactly, so this pattern is hidden in figure **b**.*

Point to figure **c**.

>*Can the outline shape of the pattern be found in figure **c**?*

Answer: No.

>*What is different?*

Answer: The vertical sides are too short and the corner diagonals are too long to fit the pattern.

>*What about the intersecting lines? Are they the same?*

Answer: No; they intersect at a different (higher) point in the figure. Cover figure **c** with the pattern.

>*The pattern is not hidden in figure **c**.*

Point to figure **d**.

>*Is the pattern hidden in figure **d**?*

Answer: No. Allow students to state why the pattern is not found, then lay the pattern over figure **d**.

>*Since neither the outline shape nor the intersecting lines match, the pattern is not hidden in figure **d**.*

GUIDED PRACTICE:
EXERCISE: **A-22**
Give students sufficient time to complete this exercise. Then, using the demonstration methodology above, have them discuss their choice, asking them to explain why the incorrect answers were eliminated. Students should darken the pattern to emphasize design. *NOTE: This figure-ground exercise is more difficult than it appears.*
ANSWER: **A-22** c

INDEPENDENT PRACTICE:
Assign exercises **A-23** through **A-30**

DISCUSSION TIPS:
Encourage students to describe patterns accurately. Some students look for **key patterns**. Ask them to describe this technique to others. Although this process may be helpful, it should be used to eliminate rather than to confirm answers. Sketching a square around the patterns may aid perception for some students.

ANSWERS:
A-23 a and d; **A-24** c; **A-25** c; **A-26** a; **A-27** d; **A-28** b; **A-29** d; **A-30** a

FOLLOW-UP REFERENT:
　　　When might you need to find or follow a line or pattern within a larger design?
Examples: reading a map; art patterns; electric circuits; furniture or clothing reproduction; unknotting a tangled chain or rope

CURRICULUM APPLICATION:
Language Arts: rhyme pattern in poetry; finding hidden words or repeated letter patterns
Mathematics: finding patterns or other shapes within geometric shapes
Science: tracing the path of blood or any system through the body
Social Studies: following or indicating a historical trip on a map, e.g., the Oregon Trail, the Pony Express route, the travels of Lewis and Clark; locating mapped boundaries
Enrichment Areas: finding repeated interval patterns in music; reproducing art projects; identifying or learning steps to a dance; recognizing or drawing pattern plays in sports or formation diagrams in marching band or drill teams

EXTENDING ACTIVITIES:
Figural Similarities, Book B-1, pp. 3–4

FINDING SHAPES

STRAND: Figural Similarities   **PAGES:** 11–13

ADDITIONAL MATERIALS:
Transparency of TM #3 (cut apart as indicated)
Piece of small furniture or clothing with obvious seams

INTRODUCTION:

Have you ever watched anyone put together a piece of clothing or furniture? He or she seems to see just how the pieces fit to become a single article. If you look closely, you can see where the pieces have been put together.

Show a piece of clothing or furniture with seams and indicate the parts of the whole.

OBJECTIVE:

In these exercises you will decide which shapes from a group are used to make a given figure.

DEMONSTRATION/EXPLANATION:

Project TM #3.

This figure...

Indicate the given figure and each component part as you explain.

...is composed of a circle, a triangle, and two connecting lines. It also contains many other shapes and figures. Which of these shapes...

Point to shapes **a**, **b**, **c**, and **d**.

...can you find in the figure? Can shape a be a part of the figure?

Place shape **a** on the corresponding pattern section.

Shape a fits exactly, so you will put a check on it to show that it is a pattern shape for this figure. Can shape b be a pattern shape?

Answer: No.

Why not?

Answer: The base is the same, but the triangle is not tall enough. Place shape **b** on the corresponding pattern section to confirm the answer, then remove it. Indicate shape **c**.

Is this a pattern shape?

Answer: Yes. Place shape **c** on the corresponding pattern section and put a check mark on it.

This piece also fits exactly. Is shape d a pattern shape?

Allow students to discuss the possibility and state their reasoning, then place shape **d** so that the arc fits the circle.

The circular part matches, but the shape is not wide enough. It is not a pattern shape for this figure.

GUIDED PRACTICE:

EXERCISE: **A-31**

Give students sufficient time to complete this exercise. Then, using the demonstration methodology above, have them discuss and explain their choices.

ANSWER: **A-31** b and c

INDEPENDENT PRACTICE:

Assign exercises **A-32** through **A-36**

DISCUSSION TIPS:

Students should know the words practiced in the first two lessons which described shapes and sizes. Emphasize the comparative terms **taller, shorter, wider, narrower, more pointed**, and encourage students to use these words with qualifiers, e.g., **slightly**

smaller, **much wider**. Students may have difficulty verbalizing these figural perceptions. These exercises contribute valuable language training only if the words are *used*, *reinforced*, and become *functional* in the learner's vocabulary.

ANSWERS:
A-32 b and c; **A-33** c, d, and e; **A-34** b and c; **A-35** b and c; **A-36** b and d

FOLLOW-UP REFERENT:
> *When might you need to recognize individual parts after something has been put together?*

Examples: art activities; parts of furniture, tools, or picture puzzles; engine or motor parts

CURRICULUM APPLICATION:
Language Arts: recognizing phonemes and/or syllables of words; recognizing
   component parts of compound words
Mathematics: identifying numerals in arithmetic problems
Science: recognizing parts of trees, plants, insects, and animals; recognizing
   components of compound materials; differentiating among skeletal parts
Social Studies: comparing shapes and sizes of countries and continents; comparing
   aerial photomaps or topographic maps with maps showing governmental divisions,
   e.g., cities, counties, states, countries
Enrichment Areas: duplicating components of an art activity; recognizing parts of a
   stanza of music, e.g., clef sign, bar, time signature; recognizing different dance steps;
   recognizing moves or patterns in sports plays

EXTENDING ACTIVITIES:
None.

COMBINING SHAPES

STRAND: Figural Similarities   **PAGES:** 14–17

ADDITIONAL MATERIALS:
Transparency of TM #4 (cut apart as indicated)
Washable transparency marker
Dress or shirt pattern

INTRODUCTION:
> *Sometimes parts don't look quite the same as you expect they should after they have been put together. When you are making a garment, for example, the pattern piece that looks like this...*

Hold up a sleeve pattern piece.
> *...becomes the part of the garment that is here.*

Indicate a sleeve.
> *It looks different as a piece than it does after it has become part of a whole garment.*

OBJECTIVE:

In these exercises you will practice recognizing what a figure will look like when individual shapes have been put together.

DEMONSTRATION/EXPLANATION:

Project TM #4. Demonstrate that the cutout shapes can be moved around, then indicate figures **a**, **b**, **c**, and **d**.

Here are four figures which might be made by combining the three given shapes. You are to determine which figures are actually composed of these shapes. To form the figures, you may turn the shapes in any direction.

Place the three shapes under figure **a**.

Can this figure be made by combining the shapes?

Answer: Yes. Confirm the answer by placing the movable shapes over their corresponding sections, then place the shapes under figure **b**.

Can this figure be made by combining the shapes?

Allow students to express opinions and state reasons for their choice. Place the movable shapes over their corresponding sections.

The rectangle shape is the same height as the rectangle in the figure, but it is narrower. This figure cannot be made by combining the shapes.

Indicate figure **c**.

Can you make this figure from the shapes?

Answer: No.

Why not?

Answer: The rectangle is the same height as the rectangle in the figure, but it is narrower. Confirm the answer with the movable shapes, then repeat the procedure for figure **d**.

Check figure d, indicating that it can be formed from the given shapes.

GUIDED PRACTICE:

EXERCISES: **A-37, A-38**

Give students sufficient time to complete these exercises. Then, using the demonstration methodology above, have them discuss and explain their choices.

ANSWERS: **A-37** b and d; **A-38** b and c

INDEPENDENT PRACTICE:

Assign exercises **A-39** through **A-43**

DISCUSSION TIPS:

Help students identify objects in the classroom which contain geometric shapes, noting how the parts appear within the whole, e.g., **ceiling** or **floor tiles**, **concrete block** or **brick walls, window panes**.

ANSWERS:

A-39 a and c; **A-40** b and c; **A-41** a and e; **A-42** b and d; **A-43** a and d

FOLLOW-UP REFERENT:

When might you need to recognize or identify how parts have been rearranged or combined to form a whole?

Examples: parts of a sandwich; pizza, apple, or orange slices; parts of a clock or motor; parts of a puzzle or tangram; electrical circuits

CURRICULUM APPLICATION:

Language Arts: recognizing word parts; preparing layouts or designs for journalism projects; constructing a format for visual aids to be used with a presentation

Mathematics: recognizing fractional parts; rearranging irregular polygons into regular shapes

Science: recognizing parts of trees, plants, insects, and animals; seeing parts of compound materials; recognizing connections between skeletal parts; assembling science apparatus

Social Studies: recognizing or finding subdivisions on maps, e.g., wards, cities, counties, states, countries, continents

Enrichment Areas: recognizing sections of orchestras or bands; art collages

EXTENDING ACTIVITIES:
None.

RECOMBINING SHAPES

STRAND: Figural Similarities   **PAGES:** 18–19

ADDITIONAL MATERIALS:
Transparencies of TM #5 and student workbook page 18
Student handouts of TM #5
Washable transparency marker
Scissors
Rulers

INTRODUCTION:
In the previous exercise you recognized which figures could be made by combining a given group of shapes.

OBJECTIVE:
In these exercises you will cut apart a shape with a single straight cut and recombine the parts to make a square.

DEMONSTRATION/EXPLANATION:
Project TM #5. Distribute copies of TM #5 and have students cut out the two T-shaped shapes at the top.
If you cut the top right section from one of the T's...
Draw a dotted vertical line on the transparency to indicate the cut line.
...can you combine the two sections you now have into a square?
Move the two sections as shown in the **EXAMPLE** on page 18.
The sections form a square. Is there another way the T can be cut and rearranged to form a square? Use your other T to find out.

Possible answers: Cut off the top left of the T and move it to the lower right corner to form a square (see **1** below); make a single vertical cut up the center of the figure, reverse one section, and recombine (see **2** below).

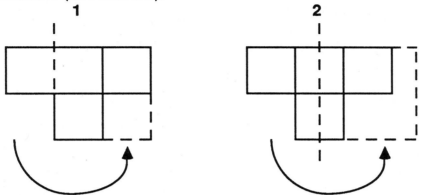

There are several ways of cutting the T and recombining the sections to form a square. Each shape on your handout can be cut with a single straight cut and recombined into a square. Practice with two or three.

Allow time for practice, drawing solutions on the transparency. Possible answers:

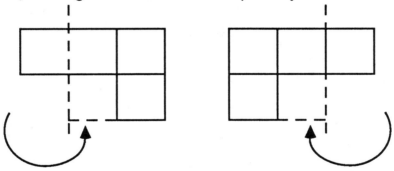

Project the transparency of page 18.

*Now, instead of cutting the shape, you are to decide how it should be cut, then draw the cut line. Where can you cut the shape in exercise **A-44** to get two sections that could be recombined into a square?*

Allow time for decision making.

You can draw any one of many vertical lines for a correct solution. You should "cut" in such a way that there are only two sections. Here are some drawing hints that will help you draw your finished square on the dot grid:

Illustrate exercise **A-44** on the answer grid as you explain each hint.

First, place your ruler along the baseline of the shape and extend a line into the grid.

Demonstrate.

Place the ruler along the top line of the shape and extend that line into the grid.

Demonstrate.

Count the number of spaces between the top and bottom guidelines.

Demonstrate.

Using the same number of spaces, sketch a square on the grid.

Each square will be six spaces high by six spaces wide. Allow time for students to draw the square.

> ***Now that you have your square drawn, sketch in the position of the "section" you "cut" from the original shape.***

Allow several students to illustrate their solutions on the transparency. Possible answer:

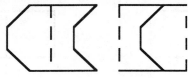

GUIDED PRACTICE:

EXERCISE: **A-45**

Give students sufficient time to complete this exercise. Then, using the demonstration methodology above, have them discuss and explain their choices. *NOTE: Many answers are possible.*

ANSWERS:

A-45

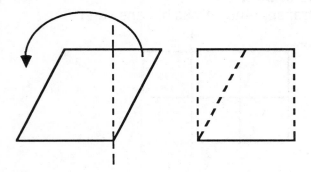

INDEPENDENT PRACTICE:

Assign exercises **A-46** through **A-48**

DISCUSSION TIPS:

Help students identify objects in the classroom which contain geometric shapes, noting how the parts appear within the whole, e.g., **ceiling** or **floor tiles**, **concrete block** or **brick walls**, **window panes**.

ANSWERS:

A-46

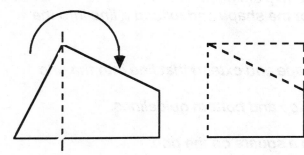

A-47   **A-48**

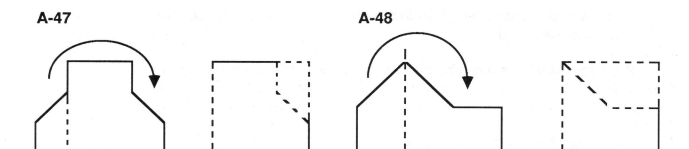

FOLLOW-UP REFERENT:

When might you need to recognize or identify how parts have been rearranged or combined to form a whole?

Examples: pizza, apple, or orange slices; parts of a clock or motor; parts of a puzzle or tangram; electrical circuits; cutting patterns and assembling finished products

CURRICULUM APPLICATION:

Language Arts: rearranging words; constructing "dummy" pages for journalism projects; deciding how to arrange lines or stanzas of original poetry

Mathematics: regrouping numerals in arithmetic problems; geometry constructions

Science: assembling science apparatus

Social Studies: map puzzles

Enrichment Areas: creating an art collage

EXTENDING ACTIVITIES:

None.

WHAT SHAPE COMPLETES THE SQUARE?

STRAND: Figural Similarities   **PAGES:** 20–21

ADDITIONAL MATERIALS:

Transparency of TM #6 (cut apart as indicated)

Markers for students (optional)

INTRODUCTION:

In previous exercises you divided shapes and discovered how important it can be to estimate visually how a shape would look if it were cut and recombined.

OBJECTIVE:

In these exercises it is also important to correctly visualize a part needed to complete a given shape. You will choose a shape which completes a square.

DEMONSTRATION/EXPLANATION:

Project TM #6. Arrange the four cutout shapes in order next to the incomplete square.

You are to determine which of these shapes completes the square. Will shape a complete the square?

Answer: No.

Why not? Both the baseline and the height seem to be about right?

Answer: The top part of **a** is too wide and will overlap the large square. Shape **a** would also leave the center of the square uncovered. Place shape **a** in the space to confirm the answer.

Will shape b complete the square?

Answer: No.

Why not?

Answer: It is too wide; both the top and bottom of **b** will overlap the large square and the center notch is going the wrong way. Place shape **b** in the space to confirm the answer.

Will shape c complete the square?

Answer: No.

Why not?

Answer: The notch fits into place, but the top and bottom sections are not wide enough. Place shape **c** in the space to confirm the answer.

Will shape d complete the square?

Answer: Yes.

How do you know?

Answer: The notch fits and the width is correct. Place shape **d** in the space to confirm the answer.

GUIDED PRACTICE:
EXERCISES: **A-49, A-50**

Give students sufficient time to complete these exercises. Then, using the demonstration methodology above, have them discuss and explain their choices.

ANSWERS:

A-49   **A-50**

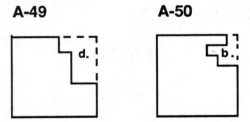

INDEPENDENT PRACTICE:
Assign exercises **A-51** through **A-53**

DISCUSSION TIPS:
Key concepts in this lesson are **completes** and **equals**. Make a list on the chalkboard of words students use to explain why the incorrect shapes did not complete the square. Students who have difficulty visualizing the shapes may find it helpful to sketch in the outline of the completed square. An optional strategy for teaching this lesson involves asking students to color the missing area of the square and the areas of the four shapes using the same color. Similarity of the colored areas may be a helpful visual cue.

ANSWERS:
A-51   **A-52**   **A-53**

   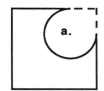

FOLLOW-UP REFERENT:
When might you need to determine what shape is needed to make an object complete?
Examples: deciding how many pieces of cake are missing; determining which puzzle piece you need; deciding what part of a model or pattern is missing

CURRICULUM APPLICATION:
Language Arts: completing journalism layout or design projects
Mathematics: geometry exercises; estimating complementary angles; confirming that the sum of the angles in a triangle is 180° by drawing a triangle, cutting the three angles at the vertices, and laying the angles next to one another to show they form a straight line
Science: deciding which bone completes a skeletal part; matching leaf or insect halves for symmetry
Social Studies: completing a map, graph, or chart; deciding where a date fits on a given time line
Enrichment Areas: choosing pattern pieces in sewing or woodworking; deciding note value to complete a measure of music; balancing artwork on a page

EXTENDING ACTIVITIES:
None.

COMPLETING THE SQUARE WITH TWO SHAPES

STRAND: Figural Similarities   **PAGES:** 22–23

ADDITIONAL MATERIALS:
Transparency of TM #7 (cut apart as indicated)
Markers for students (optional)

INTRODUCTION:
In the previous exercise you completed a square with a single shape and saw how important it was to estimate visually which part would complete the square shape correctly.

OBJECTIVE:
In these exercises you will choose and visually combine the two shapes which will complete a square.

DEMONSTRATION/EXPLANATION:

Project TM #7 (exercise **A-54**, student workbook page 22). Arrange the four cutout shapes in order next to the incomplete square.

> *You need to determine which combination of these shapes...*

Indicate the choices.

> *...will complete this square. The shapes may be turned in any direction.*

Place shape **a** in the space on the square.

> *Could shape a be one of the shapes needed to complete the square?*

Answer: Possibly.

> *Why?*

Answer: It fits in the open space in the big square. Leave shape **a** in place and move shape **b** into the remaining space.

> *Can shape b be one of the shapes needed to complete the square?*

Answer: Possibly, but not in combination with shape **a**.

> *Why?*

Answer: Shape **b** is not tall enough to fill in the remaining space, although it fits the center section. Leave shapes **a** and **b** in position and add shape **c**.

> *Can shape c be one of the shapes needed to complete the square?*

Answer: Yes.

> *Why?*

Answer: It fills the remaining space from shape **b** completely. Remove shapes **a** and **c**.

> *Can shape d be one of the shapes needed to complete the square?*

Answer: No.

> *Why?*

Answer: Regardless of how you turn it, part of the shape extends out of the large square.

> *In exercise A-54 in your workbooks, draw circles around the two shapes that complete the square. In these exercises there may be more than one pair of shapes that will combine to complete the square correctly.*

Check to see that students circled shapes **b** and **c**.

GUIDED PRACTICE:

EXERCISES: **A-55, A-56**

Give students sufficient time to complete these exercises. Then, using the demonstration methodology above, have them discuss and explain their choices.

ANSWERS:

A-55   **A-56**

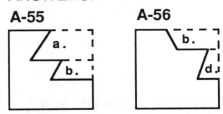

INDEPENDENT PRACTICE:

Assign exercises **A-57** through **A-59**

DISCUSSION TIPS:

Key concepts in this lesson are **completes** and **equals**. Make a list on the chalkboard of words students use to explain why the shape did not complete the square. Students who have difficulty visualizing the shapes may find it helpful to sketch in the outline of the completed square. An optional strategy for teaching this lesson involves asking students to color the missing area of the square and the areas of the four shapes using the same color. Similarity of the colored areas may be a helpful visual cue.

ANSWERS:

A-57   A-58   A-59

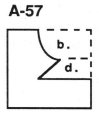   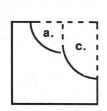 OR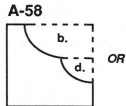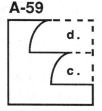

FOLLOW-UP REFERENT:

When might you need to decide which combination of shapes is needed to form a complete object?

Examples: deciding how many pieces of something is missing; determining which puzzle pieces you need; deciding what parts of a model or pattern are missing

CURRICULUM APPLICATION:

Language Arts: completing journalism layout or design projects

Mathematics: geometry exercises; estimating complementary angles; confirming that the sum of the angles in a triangle is 180° by drawing a triangle, cutting the three angles at the vertices, and laying the angles next to one another showing that they form a straight line

Science: deciding which bones complete a skeletal part; matching leaf or insect halves for symmetry

Social Studies: solving or creating map puzzles; deciding where a date fits on a given time line

Enrichment Areas: choosing pattern pieces in sewing or woodworking; deciding note value to complete a measure of music; balancing artwork on a page

EXTENDING ACTIVITIES:

None.

MATCHING CONGRUENT SHAPES

STRAND: Figural Similarities   **PAGES:** 24–25

ADDITIONAL MATERIALS:

Transparency of TM #8 (cut apart as indicated)

INTRODUCTION:

In previous exercises you saw how helpful it can be to estimate visually which part or parts were needed to make a square complete.

OBJECTIVE:
> *In these exercises you will choose two shapes that are exactly the same size and shape, although they may be facing different directions. Figures and shapes that meet this description are called* congruent.

DEMONSTRATION/EXPLANATION:
Project TM #8, cut apart and rearranged as on the transparency master.
> *You are to match each numbered triangle with the lettered triangle that is its congruent "twin." To find the congruent triangle twins, you need to describe each numbered shape, then look for a lettered shape in the second column that matches the same description. How would you describe triangle 1?*

Answer: It is a right triangle with no congruent sides. *NOTE: If necessary, draw this information from students by direct questioning regarding lines, angles, and sizes. It is important that they learn to compare the aspects of shapes and figures.*
> *Which lettered triangle fits this description?*

Answer: **b**. Pick up triangle **b** and place it over triangle **1** so all lines match.
> *Notice that triangle b had to be turned to make it match. Congruent objects do not have to face the same direction, but they must have the same shape and size.*
> *Describe triangle 2.*

Answer: It is a scalene triangle; it has one obtuse angle and no matching (congruent) sides or angles.
> *Which of the lettered triangles fits the same description?*

Answer: Triangle **c**. Place triangle **c** over triangle **2** with all sides matching.
> *Describe triangle 3.*

Answer: It is a right isosceles triangle (a right triangle with two equal sides). The height seems to be about half the length of the base.
> *Which of the remaining lettered triangles fits this description?*

Answer: Triangle **d**. Place triangle **d** over triangle **3**, with all sides matching.
> *Which of the remaining lettered triangles is congruent to triangle 4?*

Answer: Triangle **e**. Place triangle **e** over triangle **4**.
> *Are the two remaining triangles congruent?*

Answer: Yes. Place triangle **a** over triangle **5**.

GUIDED PRACTICE:
EXERCISES: **A-60, A-61, A-62, A-63, A-64**
Give students sufficient time to complete these exercises. Then, using the demonstration methodology above, have them discuss and explain their choices.
ANSWERS: **A-60** e; **A-61** b; **A-62** a; **A-63** f; **A-64** d

INDEPENDENT PRACTICE:
Assign exercises **A-65** through **A-70**

DISCUSSION TIPS:
The key concept is in this lesson is **congruent**. Students can confirm congruence by cutting or tracing shapes and figures.

ANSWERS:
A-65 c; **A-66** a; **A-67** f; **A-68** e; **A-69** d; **A-70** b

FOLLOW-UP REFERENT:
   When might you need to determine identical shapes?
Examples: replacing a missing piece of flooring, roofing, or paneling; laying carpeting; upholstering; assembling a project display; quilting and textile crafts; models or crafts which require exact replicas of pattern pieces; choosing replacement parts for engines, motors, or machinery

CURRICULUM APPLICATION:
Language Arts: recognizing identical words; arranging a letter or composition into a
   given format
Mathematics: congruency exercises in geometry
Science: repairing laboratory equipment
Social Studies: matching land or water shapes for map identification; comparing
   graphed data
Enrichment Areas: choosing pattern pieces in sewing or woodworking; art projects;
   industrial arts projects; machine repairs

EXTENDING ACTIVITIES:
Area Perception, Book A-1, pp. 39–40, 43–52

WHICH SHAPE IS NOT CONGRUENT?

STRAND: Figural Similarities   **PAGES:** 26–27

ADDITIONAL MATERIALS:
Transparency of student workbook page 26 (cut out the first shape in each row)

INTRODUCTION:
   *You have learned that congruent means shapes or figures having the same size
   and shape, but not necessarily the same position. In the previous exercise you
   matched congruent shapes.*

OBJECTIVE:
   *In these exercises you will choose the one shape that is not congruent to the other
   members of the group.*

DEMONSTRATION/EXPLANATION:
Project the transparency of page 26, with the cutout shapes at the beginning of each row.
   You are to identify which one of these shapes does not match the first shape.
Pick up the shape from the **EXAMPLE** and turn it as you overlay shapes **a** through **d**.
   Which of the shapes does not match?
Answer: **c.**

How is it different?
Answer: One of the "legs" is too wide. Indicate exercise **A-71**.
    Which of the shapes does not match?
Answer: **b**.
    How is it different?
Answer: It has one right angle and the others do not. Confirm the answer by overlaying the initial shape. Repeat the procedure for **A-72**. (Answer: **d**; one diagonal side is shorter.)

GUIDED PRACTICE:
EXERCISES: **A-73, A-74**
Give students sufficient time to complete these exercises. Then, using the demonstration methodology above, have them discuss and explain their choices.
ANSWERS: **A-73** c; **A-74** a

INDEPENDENT PRACTICE:
Assign exercises **A-75** through **A-78**

DISCUSSION TIPS:
The key concept in this lesson is **congruent**. Students can confirm congruence by cutting or tracing shapes and figures.

ANSWERS:
A-75 b; **A-76** c; **A-77** a; **A-78** d

FOLLOW-UP REFERENT:
    When might you need to decide which one in a group of shapes is different from the others?
Examples: identifying a piece of flooring, roofing, or paneling as not the same size or shape as the original; laying carpeting; upholstering; setting up a project display; avoiding errors in quilting and textile crafts; models or crafts which require exact replicas of pattern pieces

CURRICULUM APPLICATION:
Language Arts: finding misspelled words
Mathematics: geometry exercises
Science: repairing science equipment
Social Studies: map puzzles
Enrichment Areas: choosing correct pattern pieces in sewing, woodworking, or art
   projects; metal working; small engine repairs

EXTENDING ACTIVITIES:
Area Perception, Book A-1, pp. 41–42

RECOGNIZING/IDENTIFYING CONGRUENT PARTS

STRAND: Figural Similarities   **PAGES:** 28–31

ADDITIONAL MATERIALS:
Transparency of TM #9 (cut apart as indicated)
Crayons or markers for students (optional)

INTRODUCTION:
In previous exercises you matched congruent shapes and determined which in a group of shapes was not congruent. You learned that congruent shapes or figures have the same size and shape.

OBJECTIVE:
In these exercises you will recognize the congruent parts of a divided figure.

DEMONSTRATION/EXPLANATION:
Project TM #9. Show that you have movable shapes.
You are to determine if the line divides the square into congruent parts.
Place the movable shapes on top of the square.
As you can see, these movable shapes are the same as those in the uncut square.
Pick up the movable shapes and lay one on top of the other.
After one shape is turned around it fits exactly on the other. The shapes are the same size and shape; they are congruent.

GUIDED PRACTICE:
EXERCISE: **A-79**
Give students sufficient time to complete this exercise. Then, using the demonstration methodology above, have them discuss and explain their choices.
ANSWER: **A-79** a, d, f, h, and k

INDEPENDENT PRACTICE:
Assign exercises **A-80** through **A-91**

DISCUSSION TIPS:
The key concept in this lesson is **congruent**. Students can confirm congruence by cutting or tracing shapes and figures. Using color for congruent parts may be helpful (and fun) in exercises **A-81** through **A-91**.

ANSWERS:
A-80 a, b, d, f, h, i, and k

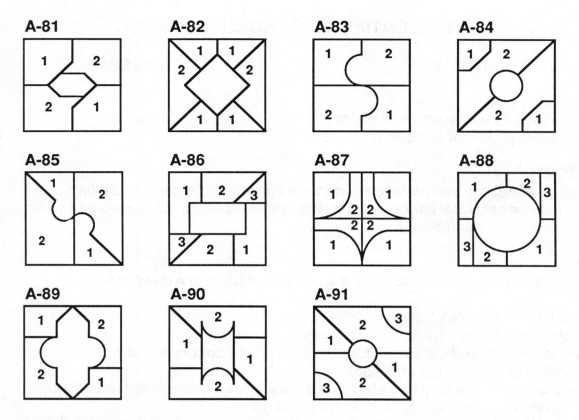

NOTE: Some students may see larger congruent figures by combining shapes. Such insights are correct and should be encouraged.

FOLLOW-UP REFERENT:
When might you need to identify identical shapes?
Examples: replacing a missing piece of flooring, roofing, or paneling; laying carpeting; upholstering; assembling a project display; quilting and textile crafts; models or crafts which require exact replicas of pattern pieces; choosing replacement parts for engines, motors, or machinery

CURRICULUM APPLICATION:
Language Arts: recognizing identical words; arranging a letter or composition into a
    given format
Mathematics: congruency exercises in geometry
Science: repairing laboratory equipment
Social Studies: matching land or water shapes for map identification; comparing
    graphed data
Enrichment Areas: choosing pattern pieces in sewing or woodworking; art projects;
    industrial art projects; machine repairs

EXTENDING ACTIVITIES:
Area Perception, Book A-1, pp. 53–54
Figural Similarities, Book A-1, pp. 22–23

DIVIDING SHAPES INTO CONGRUENT PARTS

STRAND: Figural Similarities   **PAGES:** 32–34

ADDITIONAL MATERIALS:
Transparency of TM #10
Washable transparency marker
Straightedge

INTRODUCTION:
In the previous exercise you learned to recognize whether a figure had been divided into congruent parts. This is what you are doing when you judge whether a candy bar has been evenly divided.

OBJECTIVE:
In these exercises you will divide shapes into congruent parts.

DEMONSTRATION/EXPLANATION:
Project TM #10. Use a washable marker to divide the triangular grid with a vertical line.
    If this shape is divided along this line, has it been divided into congruent parts?
Answer: No; the parts are different sizes and shapes. Have students open their workbooks to page 32. Erase your line and draw a line as shown in the **EXAMPLE**.
    Does this line divide the triangle into congruent parts?
Answer: Yes.
    Without cutting the parts, how can you make sure they are congruent?
Answer: Count the spaces along each line. If all lines are the same length, the triangles are congruent. Erase the line.
    Can you divide the first triangle in exercise A-92 into four congruent triangles?
Allow students time to complete their drawing, then have one student demonstrate his/her division on the transparency. If students have different divisions, ask each to draw them in turn on the grid, confirming that the resulting triangles are congruent. Answer:

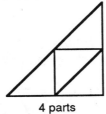
4 parts

There are many ways to divide the triangle into equal triangular parts. On the two remaining grids, divide the triangle into different congruent triangles. Count the spaces to confirm your answer. Remember, all the parts must be congruent.

GUIDED PRACTICE:
EXERCISES: remainder of **A-92, A-93**
Give students sufficient time to complete these exercises. Then, using the demonstration methodology above, have them discuss and explain their choices. Check to see that

students divided the shape correctly by discussing how to confirm whether the shapes are congruent and by counting the spaces between dots.

ANSWERS:

A-92

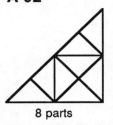

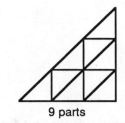

Other alternatives would include 16 or 18 triangles, produced by bisecting each triangle in the above answers.

8 parts   9 parts

A-93

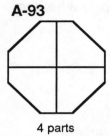   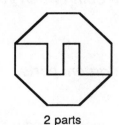   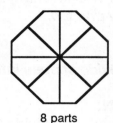   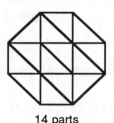

4 parts   2 parts   8 parts   14 parts

INDEPENDENT PRACTICE:
Assign exercise **A-94**

DISCUSSION TIPS:
Congruence and the process of confirming visually that parts are congruent are key concepts in this lesson. Words and phrases that mean equal, e.g., **congruent**, **same**, **symmetrical**, **as wide as**, and **as long as**, reinforce this concept. It is helpful to count spaces instead of dots. Since the dots are spaced one-fourth inch apart, it takes two dots to enclose one-quarter inch. If one counts dots, the first dot should be counted as the zero dot.

ANSWERS:
*NOTE: The parallelogram in exercise **A-94** can be divided into congruent parts in many ways, only a portion of which are shown below. Encourage students who have drawn any different or unusual divisions to draw them on the dot grid on the transparency.*

A-94

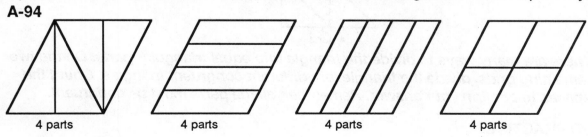

4 parts   4 parts   4 parts   4 parts

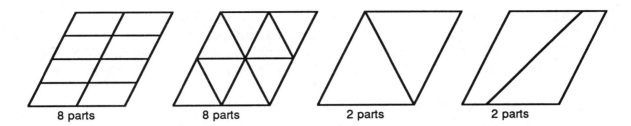

8 parts   8 parts   2 parts   2 parts

FOLLOW-UP REFERENT:
When might you need to decide whether something is divided into equal parts?
Examples: sharing food; cutting paper; constructing models or projects; paper folding; upholstering; quilting; textile crafts which involve designs to be cut on a folded edge
Why is it sometimes important to divide things equally?
Examples: fairness to others; aesthetic value; simplifying constructions or instructions

CURRICULUM APPLICATION:
Language Arts: dividing long works of literature into equal parts for several people to memorize
Mathematics: showing equal fractional parts of a whole; similarity, congruence, and symmetry exercises
Science: identifying symmetry of body parts or natural phenomena, e.g., leaves, plants, shells; dividing measurements of length, area, volume, or time into equal parts
Social Studies: dividing historical time lines into equal intervals; making or interpreting equal-interval or equal-part charts and graphs
Enrichment Areas: geometric or symmetric designs in art; measurement in home economics and industrial arts

EXTENDING ACTIVITIES:
None.

MATCHING SIMILAR SHAPES/FIGURES

STRAND: Figural Similarities   **PAGES:** 35–37

ADDITIONAL MATERIALS:
Transparencies of student workbook pages 36 and 37
Washable transparency marker

INTRODUCTION:
When you say things are similar, you mean that they are alike in some way, but not identical. For shapes or figures to be similar they must be the same shape.

OBJECTIVE:
In these exercises you will match shapes and figures that have the same shape but are not congruent.

DEMONSTRATION/EXPLANATION:
Using the transparencies as templates, produce a small triangle identical to the one in the **EXAMPLE** on page 36 and a small rectangle identical to the one in the **EXAMPLE** on page 37. Project the transparency of page 36. Use the small cutout triangle as an overlay to confirm answers.

This cutout triangle is congruent to this small triangle.
Point to the small triangle in the **EXAMPLE** and lay the cutout triangle on top to show they are congruent.

What kind of triangle is this?
Answer: A right triangle.

Are there other right triangles in the answer choice column?
Answer: Triangles **b**, **c**, and **d** are right triangles. Demonstrate the movement after each question.

*If the cutout triangle is turned to match its right angle with the right angle in triangle **d**, will these triangles be the same shape?*
Answer: No; the height of triangle **d** is much greater than its base. The height and base of the **EXAMPLE** triangle are not as different.

*If the cutout triangle is turned to match its right angle with the right angle in triangle **c**, will these triangles be the same shape?*
Answer: No; triangle **c** has two sides that are the same length.

*If the cutout triangle is turned to match its right angle with the right angle in triangle **b**, will these triangles be the same shape?*
Answer: Yes.

How can you tell that the triangles are similar?
Answer: When the two right angles are overlaid, the third side of the small triangle is parallel to the third side of the large triangle. Project the transparency of page 37. Use the small cutout rectangle.

This cutout rectangle is congruent to this small rectangle.
Point to the small rectangle in the **EXAMPLE** and lay the cutout rectangle on top to show they are congruent.

What is the size of this rectangle?
Answer: Two squares high and three squares long.

*If the cutout rectangle is moved on top of rectangle **a**, will these rectangles be the same shape?*
Answer: No; **a** is too long.

*If the cutout rectangle is moved on top of rectangle **b**, will these rectangles be the same shape?*
Answer: No; **b** is half the height of the **EXAMPLE**, but the same length.

*If the cutout rectangle is moved on top of rectangle **c**, will these rectangles be the same shape?*
Answer: No; **c** is the same height, but too long.

*If the cutout rectangle is moved on top of rectangle **d**, will these rectangles be the same shape?*
Answer: Yes.

How can you tell that the rectangles are similar?
Answer: Rectangle **d** is twice as long (six blocks) and twice as high (four blocks) as the small rectangle in the **EXAMPLE**.

GUIDED PRACTICE:
EXERCISES: **A-95, A-99**
Give students sufficient time to complete these exercises. Then, using the demonstration methodology above, have them discuss and explain their choices.
ANSWERS:
A-95 c (a right triangle with two equal sides); **A-99** e (twice as high and twice as long)

INDEPENDENT PRACTICE:
Assign exercises **A-96** through **A-98** and **A-100** through **A-103**

DISCUSSION TIPS:
Students may discover the concept that similar figures have sides that are in the same proportion. This idea will be reinforced in the exercises on **PRODUCING SIMILAR FIGURES** (pages 42–55). There is no need to emphasize the concept at this point.

ANSWERS:
A-96   e; scalene triangles
A-97   a; isosceles triangles
A-98   d; right triangles of the same shape (proportion)
A-100 b; 2 x 6 is similar to 1 x 3 (sides half as long)
A-101 c; 3 x 6 is similar to 2 x 4 (sides two-thirds as long)
A-102 a; 4 x 10 is similar to 2 x 5 (sides half as long)
A-103 f; 4 x 12 is similar to 2 x 6 (sides half as long)

FOLLOW-UP REFERENT:
> *When might you need to decide which shapes or figures in a given group are similar?*

Examples: model construction; enlarging or reducing patterns; drafting and scale drawing; project displays

CURRICULUM APPLICATION:
Language Arts: similarity of roots of different words
Mathematics: similarity and congruence exercises; recognizing equivalent fractional
    parts; mathematics problems involving the effect on area of changing the length of a
    polygon's sides
Science: determining equivalent measurement; model building
Social Studies: constructing relief maps
Enrichment Areas: drawing objects having similar shapes

EXTENDING ACTIVITIES:
None.

IDENTIFYING SIMILARITY AND CONGRUENCE—A

STRAND: Figural Similarities

PAGES: 38–39

ADDITIONAL MATERIALS:
Transparency of student workbook page 38

INTRODUCTION:
In previous exercises you identified similar and congruent shapes and figures.

OBJECTIVE:
In these exercises you will determine whether or not shapes are similar or congruent.

DEMONSTRATION/EXPLANATION:
Using the transparency as a template, produce a rectangle identical to the one in the **EXAMPLE**. Project the transparency of page 38. Use the small cutout rectangle as an overlay to confirm answers.
This cutout rectangle is congruent to the rectangle in the EXAMPLE box.
Overlay the cutout rectangle to show they are congruent.
If the cutout rectangle is placed over rectangle a, will the rectangles be the same shape?
Answer: Yes; but **a** is half as high and half as wide as the cutout rectangle. Use the overlay to confirm this answer.
Since rectangle a is half as tall and half as wide as the cutout rectangle, what can be said about rectangle a?
Answer: It is similar to the cutout rectangle.
How should rectangle a be marked to show that it is similar?
Answer: With an **S** for similar.
If the cutout rectangle is placed over rectangle b, will the rectangles be the same shape?
Answer: Yes; they match exactly.
Since rectangle b matches the cutout rectangle exactly, what can be said about rectangle b?
Answer: It is congruent to the cutout rectangle.
How should rectangle b be marked?
Answer: With a **C** for congruent.
If the cutout rectangle is placed over rectangle c, will these rectangles be the same shape?
Answer: No; **c** is the same height, but it is too wide.
Since rectangle c is the same height as the cutout rectangle but much wider, what can be said about rectangle c?
Answer: It is neither similar nor congruent to the cutout rectangle.
How should rectangle c be marked?
Answer: With an **N** for neither similar nor congruent.

GUIDED PRACTICE:
EXERCISES: **A-104, A-105**
Give students sufficient time to complete these exercises. Then, using the demonstration methodology above, have them discuss and explain their choices.
ANSWERS: **A-104** a <u>C</u>, b <u>S</u>, c <u>N</u> (too thin); **A-105** a <u>N</u> (too short), b <u>S</u>, c <u>C</u>

INDEPENDENT PRACTICE:
Assign exercises **A-106** through **A-111**

DISCUSSION TIPS:
Encourage students to explain why the shapes are or are not similar and to use comparatives, e.g., **too short** or **too tall**, **too wide** or **too narrow**.

ANSWERS:
A-106 a <u>S</u>, b <u>S</u>, c <u>C</u>;   **A-107** a <u>N</u>, b <u>N</u>, c <u>C</u>;   **A-108** a <u>N</u>, b <u>S</u>, c <u>N</u>
A-109 a <u>N</u>, b <u>C</u>, c <u>S</u>;   **A-110** a <u>C</u>, b <u>C</u>, c <u>C</u>;   **A-111** a <u>C</u>, b <u>C</u>, c <u>S</u>

FOLLOW-UP REFERENT:
When might you need to determine whether shapes or figures are similar or congruent?
Examples: model construction; enlarging or reducing patterns; drafting and scale drawing; project displays

CURRICULUM APPLICATION:
Language Arts: similar roots of different words
Mathematics: similarity and congruence exercises; recognizing equivalent fractional
   parts; mathematics problems involving the effect on area of changing the length of
   a polygon's sides
Science: determining equivalent measurement; model building
Social Studies: constructing relief maps
Enrichment Areas: drawing objects having similar shapes

EXTENDING ACTIVITIES:
None.

IDENTIFYING SIMILARITY AND CONGRUENCE—B

STRAND: Figural Similarities   **PAGES:** 40–41

ADDITIONAL MATERIALS:
Transparency of student workbook page 41
Washable transparency marker

INTRODUCTION:
In previous exercises you determined whether or not shapes were similar or congruent.

OBJECTIVE:
In these exercises you will identify pairs of similar and congruent shapes.

DEMONSTRATION/EXPLANATION:
Project the transparency of page 41. Using the transparency as a template, produce and cut out a parallelogram identical to parallelogram **a**. Use this cutout parallelogram as an overlay to confirm answers.
   This cutout parallelogram is congruent to parallelogram **a**.
Overlay the parallelograms to show they are congruent.
   If the cutout parallelogram is placed over parallelogram **b**, *will the parallelograms be the same shape?*
Answer: No, **b** is the same height as **a**, but wider.
   If the cutout parallelogram is flipped and placed over parallelogram **c**, *will the parallelograms be the same shape?*
Answer: Yes; they match exactly.
   Notice that parallelogram **a** *had to be flipped to make it match. Since parallelogram* **c** *matches parallelogram* **a** *exactly, what can be said about parallelogram* **c**?
Answer: It is congruent to parallelogram **a**.
   Notice that parallelograms **a** *and* **c** *are both four spaces high.*
Point and count.
   Also notice that each has a base that is three spaces long.
Point and count.
   Are any of the other parallelograms congruent to **a** *and* **c**?
Answer: **k**
   If the cutout parallelogram is rotated and flipped, then placed over parallelogram **k**, *will the parallelograms be the same shape?*
Answer: Yes; they match exactly.

GUIDED PRACTICE:
EXERCISES: **A-114, A-115**
Give students sufficient time to complete these exercises. Then, using the demonstration methodology above, have them discuss and explain why the shapes are similar. The dot grid is provided so dimensions of the parallelograms can be compared.
ANSWERS:
A-114 **a, c**, and **k** (3 spaces by 4 spaces); **b** and **i** (4 spaces by 4 spaces); **d** and **j** (2 spaces by 4 spaces); **f** and **h** (3 spaces by 2 spaces); **g** and **l** (1 space by 2 spaces)

A-115 **b** and **i** (4 spaces by 4 spaces) are similar to **e** (2 spaces by 2 spaces) **d** and **j** (2 spaces by 4 spaces) are similar to **g** and **l** (1 space by 2 spaces)

INDEPENDENT PRACTICE:
Assign exercises **A-112** and **A-113**

DISCUSSION TIPS:
Encourage students to explain their decisions and to name the triangles using correct geometric terminology.

ANSWERS:
A-112 **b** is congruent to **g** (right triangles); **c** is congruent to **e** (isosceles triangles)
A-113 **a** is similar to **d** and **f** (isosceles right triangles); **h** is similar to **c** and **e** (isosceles triangles)

FOLLOW-UP REFERENT:
When might you need to determine similar or congruent shapes or figures?
Examples: model construction; enlarging or reducing patterns; drafting and scale drawing; project displays

CURRICULUM APPLICATION:
Language Arts: similar roots of different words
Mathematics: similarity and congruence exercises; recognizing equivalent fractional parts; mathematics problems involving the effect on area of changing the length of a polygon's sides
Science: equivalent measurement; model building
Social Studies: constructing relief maps
Enrichment Areas: drawing objects having similar shapes

EXTENDING ACTIVITIES:
None.

PRODUCING SIMILAR SHAPES—ENLARGING

STRAND: Figural Similarities   **PAGES:** 42–47

ADDITIONAL MATERIALS:
Transparency of student workbook page 43
Washable transparency marker
Straightedge

INTRODUCTION:
Sometimes it is necessary to enlarge a drawing or sketch so it can be seen in greater detail.

OBJECTIVE:
In these exercises you will draw a shape with sides one and one-half or two times as long as a given shape.

DEMONSTRATION/EXPLANATION:
Project exercise **A-116** from the transparency of page 43.
You will use the dot grid to draw a shape with sides twice as long as the given shape. First you need to find a starting point for the enlarged shape on the grid. How do you decide where to start the drawing?
NOTE: *This is more difficult than it looks. Try sketching in a square if students do not suggest a reasonable answer.*

If you sketched a square around the original shape, what would that square's measurements be?

Answer: Three spaces by three spaces.

What size square would allow you to make a shape on the dot grid with sides twice as long?

Answer: Six spaces by six spaces. Trace in the square lightly, then count six spaces down from the top left corner and mark the starting point.

If each side of the enlarged shape is to be twice as long, how wide should the bottom of the shape be drawn?

Answer: Six spaces.

Why?

Answer: Because the sides are supposed to be twice as long. The original shape has a

three-space base and two times three spaces is six spaces. Draw the bottom of the enlarged shape from the marked starting point.

How tall is the smaller shape?

Answer: Three spaces.

How tall should the enlarged shape be; and where should the line begin on the dot grid?

Answer: Six spaces, beginning at the right end of the bottom line (where the last line stopped). Draw a vertical line six spaces long to continue the shape.

How long is this short line on the left of the small shape?

Point. Answer: One space.

How long should it be in the enlarged drawing?

Answer: Two spaces. Draw a vertical line two spaces tall starting at the left end of the baseline.

The new enlarged shape is just about finished. It has two six-space lines and one two-space line. How can you finish the drawing?

Answer: Use a straightedge to connect the end points of the two vertical lines.

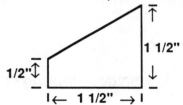

GUIDED PRACTICE:

EXERCISE: **A-117**

Give students sufficient time to complete this exercise. Then, using the demonstration methodology above, have them discuss and explain their choice. Check to see that students enlarged the shape correctly. It should be eight spaces wide and eight spaces high. If students have difficulty locating the position of the pointed part on the right, have them use the triangle rule on student workbook page 42. Starting at the top left, count four spaces over and one space down on the small shape. Starting in a similar position on the large shape, count eight spaces over and two spaces down. To check for accuracy, start at the lower left and count four spaces over and three spaces up in the small shape. Starting in a similar position on the larger shape, count eight spaces over and six spaces up to prove that you locate the same point.

ANSWER:

A-117

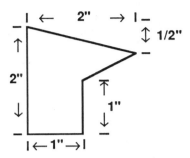

INDEPENDENT PRACTICE:

Assign exercises **A-118** through **A-127**

DISCUSSION TIPS:

When enlarging one and one-half times, have students draw a line the same length as the original line, then extend it by one-half as much. For example, a line four spaces long is copied and then extended two spaces. If students have not used the quarter-inch dot grid before, you may need to emphasize the importance of counting spaces instead of dots. If one counts dots, call the first dot zero. From the zero dot to the first dot is one space.

ANSWERS:

A-118

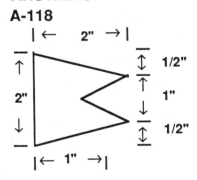

A-119

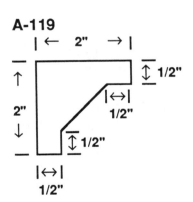

A-120

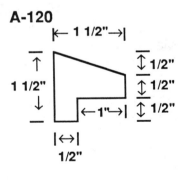

A-121

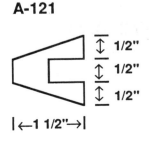

A-122

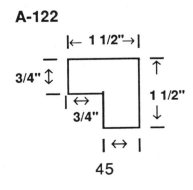

A-123

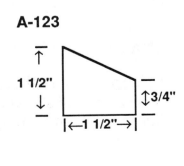

A-124

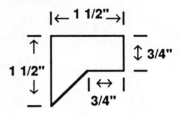

A-125

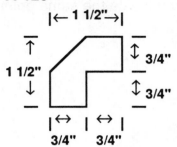

A-126

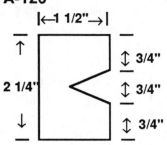

A-127

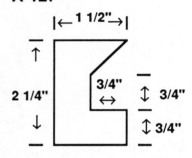

FOLLOW-UP REFERENT:
When might you need to enlarge a shape or figure proportionally?
Examples: drawing a mural; writing a sign or poster to be read from a distance; writing on a chalkboard; increasing the size of a pattern; reproducing maps or sections of maps from a smaller picture or drawing

CURRICULUM APPLICATION:
Language Arts: producing layouts from a dummy; preparing visual aids for presentations
Mathematics: copying geometric shapes using correct proportions
Science: enlarging diagrams of insects, flowers, animals; drawing images for laboratory
   reports or science fair projects
Social Studies: enlarging charts, graphs, or maps
Enrichment Areas: art projects; enlarging scale drawings in industrial arts or drafting

EXTENDING ACTIVITIES:
Figural Similarities, Book C-1, pp. 5–8, 16–17, 26–27

PRODUCING SIMILAR SHAPES—REDUCING

STRAND: Figural Similarities   **PAGES:** 48–52

ADDITIONAL MATERIALS:
Transparency of student workbook page 49
Washable transparency marker
Straightedge

INTRODUCTION:
> *In the previous exercise you enlarged a given shape to make a similar shape.*

OBJECTIVE:
> *Sometimes it is necessary to make a similar shape or figure by reducing a drawing to a more convenient size. In these exercises you will produce shapes with sides one-half or three-fourths as long as a given shape.*

DEMONSTRATION/EXPLANATION:
Project exercise **A-128** from the transparency of page 49.
> *You are to draw a shape with sides one-half as long as the given shape. First you need to determine a starting point on the dot grid for the reduced shape. Start in the top left corner.*

Mark the starting point on the grid.
> *How long is the top line of the given shape?*

Answer: Eight spaces.
> *If the reduced shape is to have sides one-half as long, how wide should you draw the top of your reduced shape?*

Answer: Four spaces.
> *Why?*

Answer: Because each side is supposed to be one-half as long and one-half of eight spaces is four spaces. Draw the top of the reduced shape.
> *How tall is the left side of the given shape?*

Answer: Four spaces.
> *How tall should the corresponding side of the reduced shape be?*

Answer: Two spaces.
> *Where should the line begin on the drawing?*

Answer: On the left end of the first line. Draw the left vertical line.
> *How long is the shorter line on the right of the large shape?*

Point. Answer: Two spaces.
> *How long should this line be in the reduced drawing?*

Answer: One space. Draw the right-side vertical line one space tall. Continue the dialogue, adding the correct one-space-long lines to produce the final reduced shape.

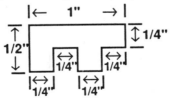

GUIDED PRACTICE:
EXERCISE: **A-129**
Give students sufficient time to complete this exercise. Then, using the demonstration methodology above, have them discuss and explain their choice. Check students' drawings or have them reproduce their drawings on the transparency.

ANSWER:
A-129

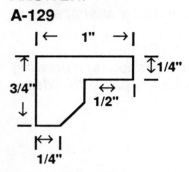

INDEPENDENT PRACTICE:
Assign exercises **A-130** through **A-139**

DISCUSSION TIPS:
As an alternative to the **EXAMPLE** on student workbook page 48 (reducing a shape so its sides are three-fourths as long) it may be helpful to have students count the spaces on the larger shape in groups of four. Each group of four spaces would then be reproduced as a group of three spaces. For example, a line eight spaces long is counted as two four-space groups and reproduced as two three-space groups. If students have not used the quarter-inch dot grid before, you may need to emphasize the importance of counting spaces instead of dots. If one counts dots, call the first dot zero. From the zero dot to the first dot is one space.

ANSWERS:

A-130

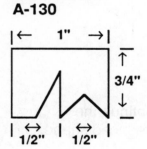

A-131

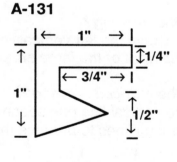

A-132

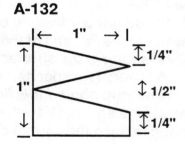

A-133

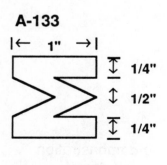

A-134

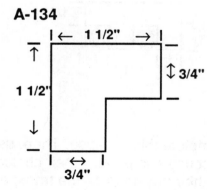

A-135

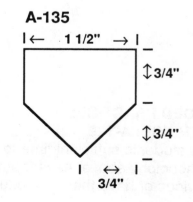

A-136

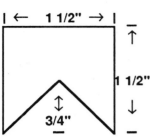

A-137

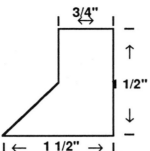

A-138

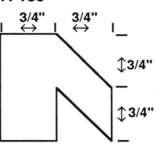

A-139

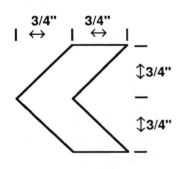

FOLLOW-UP REFERENT:

When might you need to reduce a shape or figure proportionally?

Examples: copying a large map or chart to paper; copying notes or illustrations from a chalkboard or projection screen; scale drawings; model or miniature constructions

CURRICULUM APPLICATION:

Language Arts: producing dummy layouts for newspapers or advertisements
Mathematics: reducing geometric shapes using correct proportions; similarity and
  congruence exercises; sketching ratio and proportion problems
Science: reducing diagrams of natural objects
Social Studies: reducing charts, graphs, or maps
Enrichment Areas: art projects; scale drawings in industrial arts or drafting; drawing
  dance-step patterns; charting pattern plays in sports; reducing or cropping graphics

EXTENDING ACTIVITIES:

Figural Similarities, Book C-1, pp. 9–14, 18–21

IDENTIFYING ENLARGEMENT AND REDUCTION

STRAND: Figural Similarities   **PAGES:** 53–55

ADDITIONAL MATERIALS:

Transparency of student workbook page 53
Washable transparency marker

INTRODUCTION:
In previous exercises you enlarged or reduced shapes by a given factor.

OBJECTIVE:
In these exercises you will identify whether a shape has been enlarged or reduced and determine the enlargement or reduction factor.

DEMONSTRATION/EXPLANATION:
Project the **EXAMPLE** from the transparency of page 53.
Is shape B larger or smaller than shape A?
Answer: Larger.
If shape B is larger than shape A, would you say it has been enlarged or reduced?
Answer: Enlarged.
You are also to determine the factor of enlargement. What length are the baselines of these two shapes?
Answer: The base of shape **A** is four spaces long; the base of shape **B** is six spaces long.
Compare the baselines of the two . How can you compare the new size to the original size?
Answer: Divide the new length (the base of **B**) by the original length (the base of **A**).
The answer you obtained is called the enlargement factor. You can say that shape B has been enlarged by a factor of one and one-half. Has each side of the enlarged shape been changed in the same way?
Answer: Yes. Project exercise **A-140**.
Is shape B larger or smaller than shape A?
Answer: Smaller.
Would you say it has been enlarged or reduced?
Answer: Reduced. Write <u>REDUCED</u> in the first blank.
Compare the corresponding sides and compute the reduction factor.
Answer: The original shape is four spaces wide and four spaces tall; the reduced shape is three spaces wide and three spaces tall. The reduction factor is three-fourths (three divided by four).

GUIDED PRACTICE:
EXERCISE: **A-141**
Give students sufficient time to complete this exercise. Then, using the demonstration methodology above, have them discuss and explain their choice.
ANSWER: **A-141** Each side of figure **B** has been <u>enlarged</u> to <u>2</u> times as long.

INDEPENDENT PRACTICE:
Assign exercises **A-142** through **A-147**

DISCUSSION TIPS:
Some students have difficulty expressing the enlargement or reduction factor. For example, they may compute a two-to-one ratio and then say the shape is <u>reduced</u> to <u>two</u> times as long, instead of <u>one-half</u> times as long. If students repeat their answers aloud, they can often hear their error.

ANSWERS:

A-142 Each side of shape B has been <u>enlarged</u> to <u>2</u> times as long.

A-143 Each side of shape B has been <u>reduced</u> to <u>1/2</u> times as long.

A-144 Each side of shape B has been <u>enlarged</u> to <u>2</u> times as long.

A-145 Each side of shape B has been <u>reduced</u> to <u>1/2</u> times as long.

A-146 Each side of shape B has been <u>enlarged</u> to <u>1 1/2</u> times as long.

A-147 Each side of shape B has been <u>reduced</u> to <u>3/4</u> times as long.

FOLLOW-UP REFERENT:

When might you need to recognize and determine enlargement or reduction factors?

Examples: enlarging or reducing photographs; using a proportion wheel to crop photos or graphics; recognizing scaling factors in drafting or model construction; enlarging or reducing patterns; project displays

CURRICULUM APPLICATION:

Language Arts: producing newspaper or advertisement layouts; identifying type sizes

Mathematics: copying geometric shapes; fractions; ratio and proportion problems; problems involving the effect on area or volume when changing the length of the sides of polygons or solids; estimating measurements

Science: recognizing organism or crystal growth; measuring material

Social Studies: interpreting map scales; interpreting bar or pie charts for comparative information

Enrichment Areas: art projects involving size change; recognizing size change in home economics and industrial arts materials; enlarging, reducing, or proportioning photograph prints

EXTENDING ACTIVITIES:

Figural Similarities, Book C-1, pp. 21–23

USING DIFFERENT-SIZED GRIDS TO ENLARGE OR REDUCE FIGURES

STRAND: Figural Similarities   **PAGES:** 56–59

ADDITIONAL MATERIALS:

Transparency of student workbook page 56
Washable transparency marker
Straightedge

INTRODUCTION:

In the previous exercise you identified whether a shape had been enlarged or reduced and determined the enlargement or reduction factor.

OBJECTIVE:

In these exercises you will enlarge or reduce figures by using different-sized grids.

DEMONSTRATION/EXPLANATION:

Project the **EXAMPLE** from the transparency of page 56.

> *Have you ever watched a painter copy a small picture to a large painting? One of the first steps is determining a starting point so the new copy will fit into the drawing area. How can you decide where to begin this drawing on the enlarged grid?*

Answer: Count the spaces in the width and height of the smaller picture.

> *How wide is the small boat?*

Answer: Five spaces.

> *How tall is the small boat?*

Answer: Four spaces.

> *Make a light outline on the larger grid just outside an area five spaces wide and four spaces high. This will be the "frame" for your enlarged drawing.*

Sketch this on the transparency.

> *How long is the bottom of the boat and where does it begin?*

Answer: It is two spaces long and begins one space in from the left side on the bottom row. Draw the corresponding line on the larger grid.

> *On the original figure, how many spaces above the bottom line is the widest part of the boat?*

Answer: One space. Draw the longer horizontal line on the transparency.

> *Now locate the position for the top of the boat. How far is it above the baseline?*

Answer: Four spaces.

> *How far in is the top point from the left edge of the drawing?*

Answer: Two spaces. Draw the vertical line on the transparency.

> *Notice that the bottom of the sail does not pass through any grid points. How can you locate this line?*

Answer: By estimating that it is one and one-half spaces above the baseline and three spaces long. Draw the line.

> *Now you can complete the enlarged drawing by connecting the corresponding end points. Use a straightedge to place the diagonals.*

Give students time to complete the drawing.

> *In exercise A-148, what are the outside measurements of the lamp?*

Answer: Four spaces wide and five spaces high. Sketch the outline of the area on the transparency.

> *Where should the top center point of the lamp shade be located?*

Answer: Two spaces in from the left edge. Mark this point with an X.

> *Now that you have located some of the important points, complete the enlarged drawing. You will need to estimate the measurements of the lamp base.*

GUIDED PRACTICE:

EXERCISE: remainder of **A-148**
Give students sufficient time to complete this exercise. Then, using the demonstration methodology above, have them discuss and explain their drawings.
ANSWER: **A-148** Check students' drawings.

INDEPENDENT PRACTICE:

Assign exercises **A-149** through **A-153**

DISCUSSION TIPS:

There are three simple ways to enlarge or reduce patterns: change the number of units, change the size of the grid, or, if exact scaling factor is not important, use an opaque projector to enlarge drawings (or an overhead projector to enlarge outline shapes). Encourage students to use these techniques in displays or projects and allow them to observe the use of these techniques in creating bulletin boards, theatrical scenery, or murals. This activity becomes an excellent math lab exercise. Give students a selection of several types of graph paper with different-sized grids and ask them to reconstruct the same drawing, colored the same way with felt tip pens. This demonstrates graphically the ease with which students can change drawings to fit whatever scale is desired.

ANSWERS:

Check students' drawings.

FOLLOW-UP REFERENT:

When might you need to enlarge or reduce a figure or drawing proportionally?
Examples: constructing scale models or miniatures; using patterns which require enlargement or reduction; project displays

CURRICULUM APPLICATION:

Language Arts: producing dummy pages or layouts for newspapers or advertisements
Mathematics: copying geometric shapes; similarity exercises; fraction, ratio, and
    proportion problems; estimating the effect on area or volume when changing the length
    of the sides in polygons or solids
Science: enlarging or reducing diagrams of natural phenomena
Social Studies: enlarging or reducing maps, charts, or graphs
Enrichment Areas: drafting or scale drawing exercises in industrial arts; art projects
    involving enlarging or reducing

EXTENDING ACTIVITIES:

None.

RECOGNIZING LINES OF SYMMETRY

STRAND: Figural Similarities   **PAGES:** 60–61

ADDITIONAL MATERIALS:

Transparency of TM #11
Student handouts of TM #11
Scissors for students
Washable transparency marker

INTRODUCTION:

In previous exercises you learned to recognize congruent parts of shapes and figures.

OBJECTIVE:
In these exercises you will recognize lines of symmetry. A line of symmetry divides a shape or figure into mirror image congruent parts.

DEMONSTRATION/EXPLANATION:
Project TM #11. Distribute copies of TM #11 and scissors.
It is possible for a line to divide a shape into congruent parts and not be a line of symmetry. The test for a line of symmetry involves folding—not cutting or turning or flipping. If a shape has a line of symmetry, you can fold the shape on the line and the two parts will fit exactly on top of each other. Cut out shape a and fold it along the line.
Allow time for cutting and folding.
Do the parts fit exactly on top of each other?
Answer: Yes.
Since folding the shape on the line makes two parts that fit each other exactly, the drawn line is a line of symmetry for that shape. Cut out shape b and fold it along the line to see if the parts fit exactly on one another.
Allow time for cutting and folding.
Do the parts fit exactly?
Answer: No; the left side is larger.
The line drawn in shape b is not a line of symmetry. Look at shape c. If it were folded along the line, do you think the parts would fit exactly on top of one another? Cut and fold the shape to confirm your prediction.
Allow time for cutting and folding.
Do the parts fit exactly?
Answer: Yes.
Is the drawn line a line of symmetry?
Answer: Yes.
Now look at shape d. Is the drawn line a line of symmetry?
Answer: No; the parts have the same area, but different shapes.

GUIDED PRACTICE:
EXERCISE: **A-154**
Give students sufficient time to complete this exercise. Then, using the demonstration methodology above, have them discuss and explain their choices.
ANSWER:
A-154 a yes; **b** yes; **c** no (the right side is too large); **d** no (the parts have different shapes); **e** no (the right side is too small); **f** no (the parts have different shapes); **g** yes

INDEPENDENT PRACTICE:
Assign exercise **A-155**

DISCUSSION TIPS:
Encourage students to explain their answers.

ANSWERS:
A-155 a no (the parts have different shapes); **b** no (the top is much larger); **c** yes;
d yes; **e** no (the right side is larger); **f** yes; **g** no (the parts have different shapes);
h yes; **i** no (When the shape is folded, the two parts do not lie on top of one another; the parts are congruent, but have to be turned in order to fit. In testing for symmetry, the parts are produced by folding, but are not movable)

FOLLOW-UP REFERENT:
  When might you need to recognize a line of symmetry?
Examples: observing symmetry as a design principle, e.g., airplane and automobile construction, Mexican tile patterns, American Indian craft design, clothing construction

CURRICULUM APPLICATION:
Language Arts: ——————
Mathematics: observing symmetry as a concrete example of equality in mathematics
 and as a principle in geometry
Science: observing symmetry in natural forms in biological and physical sciences
Social Studies: observing symmetry as an aesthetic value in cultures which utilize
 balance, e.g. Greeks, American Indians, American colonial architecture, Oriental
 art forms
Enrichment Areas: design principle in art, industrial arts, and home economics

EXTENDING ACTIVITIES:
None.

DRAWING LINES OF SYMMETRY

STRAND: Figural Similarities   **PAGES:** 62–63

ADDITIONAL MATERIALS:
Transparency of TM #12
Student handouts of TM #12
Scissors and straightedges for students
Washable transparency marker

INTRODUCTION:
 In the previous exercise you recognized lines of symmetry.

OBJECTIVE:
 In these exercises you will determine which shapes have lines of symmetry, then draw the lines of symmetry. Remember, a line of symmetry divides a given shape or figure into two mirror image congruent parts.

DEMONSTRATION/EXPLANATION:
Project TM #12. Distribute copies of TM #12, scissors, and straightedges.

Cut out shape a and see if you can fold it so the two parts fit exactly.

Allow time for cutting and folding, then have a student use a straightedge to draw the line of symmetry (the fold line) on the transparency.

Notice that the line of symmetry (fold line) for this shape is vertical. Cut out shape b and see if you can fold it so the parts fit exactly.

Allow time for cutting and folding, then have a student draw the line of symmetry (the fold line) on the transparency.

Notice that the line of symmetry (fold line) is horizontal this time. Look at shape c. Do you think you can fold it so the parts fit exactly? Cut out the shape and verify your prediction.

Allow time for cutting and folding.

Is it possible to fold this shape into congruent parts?

Answer: No. Cross out the shape on the transparency.

In these exercises, you will cross out any shapes that have no line of symmetry. Cut out shape d and see if you can fold it so the parts fit exactly.

Allow time for cutting and folding, then have a student draw the line of symmetry.

What direction is the line of symmetry?

Answer: Horizontal.

GUIDED PRACTICE:

EXERCISE: **A-156**

Give students sufficient time to complete this exercise. Then, using the demonstration methodology above, have them discuss and explain their choices.

ANSWER:

A-156

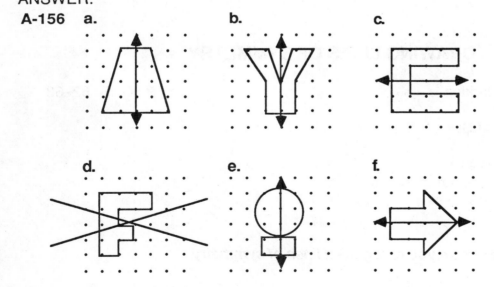

INDEPENDENT PRACTICE:

Assign exercise **A-157**

DISCUSSION TIPS:

Encourage students to use the dot grid for locating the line of symmetry and to explain their answers.

ANSWERS:
A-157

a. b. c.

d. e. f.

g. h. i.

FOLLOW-UP REFERENT:
When might you need to determine if an object has a line of symmetry and indicate the line?
Examples: observing symmetry as a design principle, e.g., airplane and automobile construction, Mexican tile patterns, American Indian craft design, clothing construction

CURRICULUM APPLICATION:
Language Arts: ————————
Mathematics: observing symmetry as a concrete example of equality in mathematics and as a principle in geometry
Science: observing symmetry in natural forms in biological and physical sciences
Social Studies: observing symmetry as an aesthetic value in cultures which utilize balance, e.g., Greeks, American Indians, American colonial architecture, Oriental art forms
Enrichment Areas: design principle in art, industrial arts, and home economics; producing symmetrical forms or letters; determining center points and setting margins in typing exercises

EXTENDING ACTIVITIES:
None.

PRODUCING SYMMETRICAL SHAPES

STRAND: Figural Similarities   **PAGES:** 64–65

ADDITIONAL MATERIALS:
Transparency of TM #13
Student handouts of TM #13
Scissors for students
Washable transparency marker

INTRODUCTION:
In the previous exercise you determined and drew lines of symmetry.

OBJECTIVE:
In these exercises you will draw the missing half of a symmetrical shape. Remember, a line of symmetry divides a shape or figure into two mirror image congruent parts.

DEMONSTRATION/EXPLANATION:
Project TM #13. Distribute copies of TM #13 and scissors.
Look at shape A. If the arrow line is to be a line of symmetry, you need to produce a congruent mirror image of the shape shown to the right of the line. How far does the top line of the shape extend from the arrow line?
Answer: Four spaces to the right.
How could you locate a corresponding end point on the left side of the line?
Answer: Count four spaces to the left, beginning at the intersection of the top of the shape and the arrow line. Mark the point on the transparency.
Now look at the bottom. To what point has the shorter diagonal line been drawn?
Answer: Two spaces to the right of the line and up one space.
How can you locate a corresponding point on the left side of the line of symmetry?
Answer: Count two spaces to the left of the intersection of the bottom line and the arrow line, then one space up. Mark the point on the transparency.
Look at the top right corner. To what point has the longer diagonal been drawn?
Answer: Three spaces down from the end point of the top line and two spaces to the left.
Starting at the top left corner, how would you find the corresponding end point of this diagonal on the left side of the line of symmetry?
Answer: Three spaces down and two spaces to the right. Mark the point.
See if you can complete the symmetrical drawing.
Allow time for students to complete the drawing.
How can you verify your drawing?
Answer: Cut out the finished drawing and fold it along the given line of symmetry to check that the two halves match. Allow time for cutting and verifying, then indicate shape **B**.
This shape has a horizontal line of symmetry. To what point has the longer diagonal been drawn?
Answer: From the right end count up three spaces and two spaces to the left.
How would you locate a corresponding point below the line of symmetry?

Answer: Count down three spaces from the intersection of the diagonal and the line of symmetry, then two spaces to the left.

> **Now that you have located a corresponding point, continue your drawing. Cut out and fold your finished drawing to verify your work.**

Allow time for completion and discussion. This task is more difficult than it appears.

GUIDED PRACTICE:
EXERCISES: **A-158, A-159**
Give students sufficient time to complete these exercises. Then, using the demonstration methodology above, have them discuss and explain their choices.
ANSWERS:

A-158   **A-159**

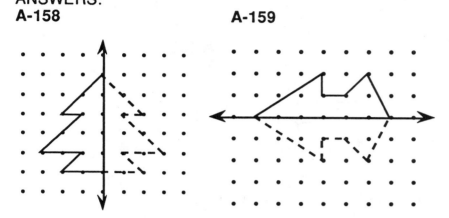

INDEPENDENT PRACTICE:
Assign exercises **A-160** through **A-168**

DISCUSSION TIPS:
Encourage students to use the dot grid for locating corresponding points and to explain their answers.

ANSWERS:
*NOTE: Students may have difficulty with **A-167** and **A-168** since the line of symmetry is diagonal. You may wish to make a transparency of this page and demonstrate how one counts out from the line of symmetry, e.g., **A-167**: Starting from the top, draw a line down two spaces, then right one space, then down two spaces, and then right three spaces.*

A-160   **A-161**   **A-162**

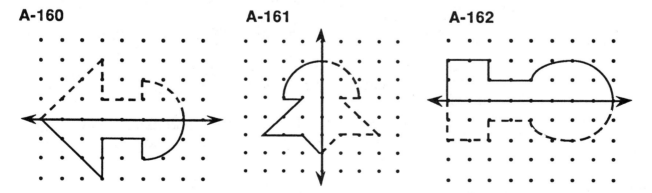

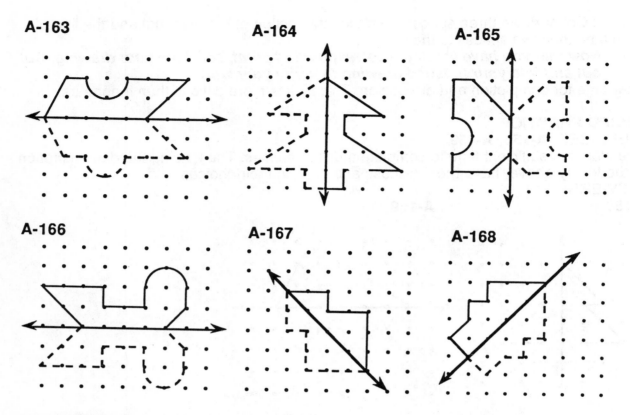

FOLLOW-UP REFERENT:

When might you use the ability to complete or visualize a symmetrical drawing or object?

Examples: symmetry as a principle of design, e.g., airplane and automobile construction, Mexican tile patterns, American Indian craft design, construction projects; origami constructions; describing symmetrical designs

CURRICULUM APPLICATION:

Language Arts: ——————

Mathematics: producing symmetrical shapes or figures as concrete examples of equality in mathematics and as a geometric principle; plotting corresponding positive and negative values on a number-value matrix; programming instructions for designing computer-generated symmetrical figures

Science: plotting paths for projectiles; drawing symmetrical objects from nature for projects or reports

Social Studies: producing symmetrical project designs for displaying the handiwork of cultures which value balance, e.g., Greeks, American Indians, American colonial architecture, Oriental art forms

Enrichment Areas: design projects in art, industrial arts, drafting, and home economics; producing symmetrical forms or letters; determining center points and setting margins in typing exercises

EXTENDING ACTIVITIES:

None.

DRAWING MULTIPLE LINES OF SYMMETRY

STRAND: Figural Similarities   **PAGES:** 66–67

ADDITIONAL MATERIALS:
Transparency of TM #14 (cut apart as indicated)
Cutout paper replicas of the three shapes for teacher use
Student handouts of TM #14
Scissors for students
Washable transparency marker

INTRODUCTION:
In the previous exercise you drew the missing half of a symmetrical shape.

OBJECTIVE:
In these exercises you will draw in all the lines of symmetry that you can find. Some shapes or figures may have more than one line of symmetry; others none.

DEMONSTRATION/EXPLANATION:
Project TM #14 (**EXAMPLES**, student workbook page 66). Distribute copies of TM #14 and scissors. Hold up the cutout triangle.
   Notice that all sides of this triangle are the same length. What kind of triangle is it?
Answer: Equilateral.
   Can an equilateral triangle be folded so the folded halves match exactly? Cut the triangle out of your copy and fold it.
Allow time for cutting and folding, then ask a student to mark a fold line on the transparency.
   What is this fold line called?
Answer: A line of symmetry.
   Did anyone find a line of symmetry different from the one drawn on the transparency?
Ask student volunteers to draw additional lines of symmetry. Have students verify each suggested line by folding their triangles.
   How many lines of symmetry does the equilateral triangle have?
Answer: Three. Repeat the above procedure with the other two shapes on the page.

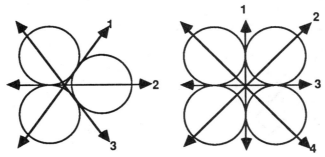

GUIDED PRACTICE:

EXERCISE: **A-169**

Give students sufficient time to complete this exercise. Then, using the demonstration methodology above, have them discuss and explain their choices.

ANSWER:

A-169

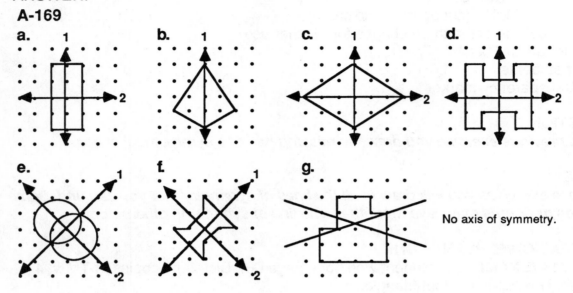

No axis of symmetry.

INDEPENDENT PRACTICE:

Assign exercise **A-170**

DISCUSSION TIPS:

Encourage students to produce and fold paper models as a test for symmetry. Patterns which have multiple lines of symmetry are described as **quadrilaterally symmetrical** if folding along <u>both</u> the horizontal and vertical axes results in all edges matching. Patterns which have multiple lines of symmetry are described as **radially symmetrical** if the pattern results from folding along multiple lines of symmetry not divisible by four, e.g., two, three, five, six, seven, nine. Radial symmetry examples appear in the daisy petal patterns and many other flower species which have three, five, or six lines of symmetry.

ANSWERS:

A-170

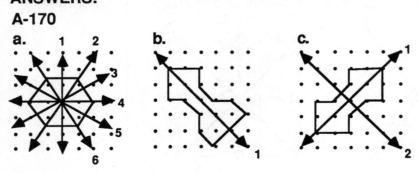

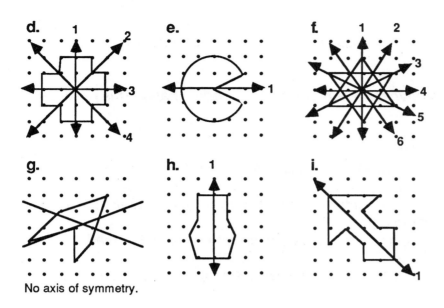

No axis of symmetry.

FOLLOW-UP REFERENT:
When might you need to determine and/or provide multiple lines of symmetry?
Examples: observing quadrilateral or radial symmetry as a principle of design, e.g., Mexican tile patterns, American Indian craft design, Oriental rugs

CURRICULUM APPLICATION:
Language Arts: producing or designing symmetrical layouts for journalism or other language arts display projects
Mathematics: producing quadrilateral symmetry as a geometric principle; plotting corresponding positive and negative values on a number-value matrix; programming instructions for computer-generated quadrilaterally or radially symmetrical figures
Science: recognizing radially symmetrical support systems in plants and buildings
Social Studies: producing quadrilaterally symmetrical designs for projects; recognizing artifacts and handiwork of cultures that value quadrilaterally and radially symmetrical patterns, e.g., American Indians, Oriental, Islamic, and Chinese art forms, Gothic vaults
Enrichment Areas: design projects in art, industrial arts and home economics; quilting, needlework, or weaving patterns with quadrilateral or radial symmetry

EXTENDING ACTIVITIES:
None.

COVERING A SURFACE

STRAND: Figural Similarities   **PAGES:** 68–70

ADDITIONAL MATERIALS:
Transparency of TM #15 (cut apart as indicated)
Student handouts of TM #15
Scissors for students
Washable transparency marker

INTRODUCTION:
In previous exercises you divided shapes and figures into congruent parts.

OBJECTIVE:
In these exercises you will cover an entire surface with equal parts. This process is known as tessellation.

DEMONSTRATION/EXPLANATION:
Project TM #15. Distribute copies of TM #15 and scissors. Slide the small pattern around the dot grid to show that it is movable.
You will use this small shape as a pattern to see if shapes this size will fit next to one another to cover the whole grid.
Start with the pattern in the top left corner; mark the outline with a washable marker; then slide the pattern to the top right corner.
How must the pattern be turned to make it fit across the top of the dot grid?
Pause for student suggestions.
Sketch in the pattern on your sheets.
Allow time for students to draw in the pattern on their handouts.
How many patterns are needed to cover the surface?
Answer: Four.
Is it possible to cover the surface by turning the pattern other ways?
Answer: Yes.
Sketch in the pattern a second way.
Answer:

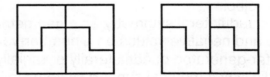

GUIDED PRACTICE:
EXERCISE: **A-171**
Give students sufficient time to complete this exercise. Then, using the demonstration methodology above, have them discuss and explain their choices. Make sure that students cover the surface completely and exacytly, with no gaps or overlaps. Many alternatives are possible; have students sketch unique solutions on the transparency.
ANSWER:

A-171

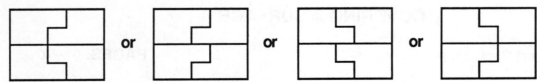

INDEPENDENT PRACTICE:
Assign exercises **A-172** through **A-177**

DISCUSSION TIPS:

If students have trouble visualizing the process, encourage them to trace the pattern, cut it out, and move it about as was done in the demonstration. It is helpful to count spaces instead of dots when using the dot grid. The dots are spaced one-half inch apart. If one counts dots, the first dot should be counted as the zero dot.

ANSWERS:

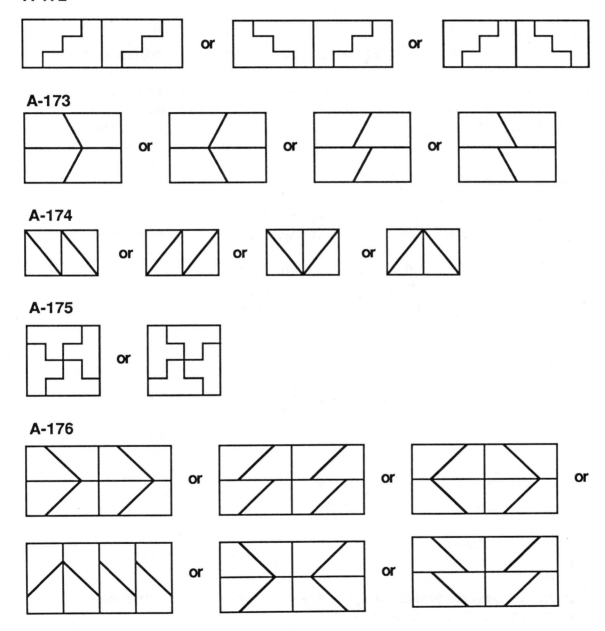

A-172

A-173

A-174

A-175

A-176

A-177

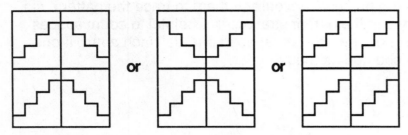

FOLLOW-UP REFERENT:

When might you need to determine how to cover a surface completely with a given shape?

Examples: installing floor or ceiling tiles, wall paneling, bricks, concrete blocks, siding, roofing; techniques used in highway or building construction; quilting patterns; designing packaging materials; spatial games such as pentominoes; minimizing waste when cutting patterns

CURRICULUM APPLICATION:

Language Arts: —————————

Mathematics: exercises in tessellation; area problems

Science: observing tessellations in biological and physical science, e.g., honeycombs, eye segmentation, crystal growth

Social Studies: estimating comparative sizes of geographic areas or features

Enrichment Areas: the art of Maurits Escher; art exercises involving positive and negative space; proportioning art or pictures to fit given areas in newspaper or yearbook layouts

EXTENDING ACTIVITIES:

None.

PRODUCING SIMILAR FIGURES BY TESSELLATION

STRAND: Figural Similarities   **PAGES:** 71–72

ADDITIONAL MATERIALS:

Transparency of TM #16 (cut apart as indicated)

Student handouts of TM #16

Scissors for students

Washable transparency marker

INTRODUCTION:

In the previous exercise you used a process known as tessellation to cover different surfaces with congruent shapes.

OBJECTIVE:

Sometimes a shape will tessellate to form a larger figure that has a similar shape. In these exercises you will test a number of shapes to see if they can reproduce themselves by tessellation.

DEMONSTRATION/EXPLANATION:
Distribute copies of TM #16 and scissors. Have students cut out the shapes.

Using the four equilateral triangles, see if you can tessellate them to produce a large equilateral triangle.

Students should work independently. When they finish, have one of them lay the pattern on the overhead projector. Answer:

Now see if you can tessellate the four diamonds to produce a larger diamond.

Students should work independently. Lay the pattern on the overhead projector. Answer:

GUIDED PRACTICE:
EXERCISES: **A-178, A-179**
Give students sufficient time to complete these exercises. Then, using the demonstration methodology above, have them discuss and explain their choices. Check students' work and have them demonstrate their drawings.
ANSWERS:

A-178

Yes; four diamonds will tessellate to form a large diamond.

A-179

Yes; four parallelograms produce a similar parallelogram. Two parallelograms produce a nonsimilar parallelogram.

INDEPENDENT PRACTICE:
Assign exercises **A-180** through **A-184**

DISCUSSION TIPS:
Encourage students to produce paper models to test their designs.

ANSWERS:

A-180   A-181   A-182   A-183   A-184

    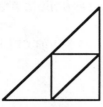   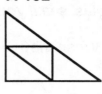   

Isosceles trapezoids will not tessellate to produce another.

Yes; four right isosceles triangles.

Yes; four right triangles.

No; a hexagon will tessellate but will not produce another hexagon.

Yes; four irregular (scalene) triangles.

FOLLOW-UP REFERENT:
When might you need to determine if a shape will cover a surface completely?
Examples: installing floor or ceiling tiles, wall paneling, bricks, concrete blocks, siding, roofing; techniques used in highway or building construction; quilting patterns; design of packaging materials; minimizing waste when cutting patterns

CURRICULUM APPLICATION:
Language Arts: ————————
Mathematics: exercises in tessellation; area problems
Science: observing tessellation in biological and physical science, e.g., honeycombs, eye segmentation, crystal growth
Social Studies: estimating relative sizes of geographic areas or features
Enrichment Areas: the art of Maurits Escher; art exercises involving positive and negative space; proportioning art or pictures to fit given areas in newspaper or yearbook layouts

EXTENDING ACTIVITIES:
None.

DRAWING TESSELLATING PATTERNS

STRAND: Figural Similarities   **PAGES:** 73–74

ADDITIONAL MATERIALS:
Transparency of student workbook page 73
Washable transparency marker

INTRODUCTION:
In previous exercises you practiced filling rectangles and producing similar shapes using tessellation.

OBJECTIVE:
In these exercises you will determine whether you can fill a hexagon with given tessellating shapes.

DEMONSTRATION/EXPLANATION:

Project exercise **A-185** from the transparency of page 73.

> ***See if you can fill this hexagon with equilateral triangles.***

Allow time for student demonstration and explanation. Answer: Yes; six equilateral triangles.

GUIDED PRACTICE:

EXERCISE: **A-186**

Give students sufficient time to complete this exercise. Then, have them demonstrate, discuss, and explain their choice.

ANSWER:

A-186

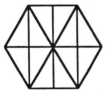

Yes; twelve right triangles.

INDEPENDENT PRACTICE:

Assign exercises **A-187** through **A-189**

DISCUSSION TIPS:

Encourage students to produce paper models to test their designs. Alternate answers are possible. Given answers indicate the fewest possible divisions.

ANSWERS:

A-187

Yes; three diamonds.

A-188

No; there will be a number of triangles and quadrilaterals left over.

A-189

Three hexagons with sides half as long are the largest hexagons that will fit. In this limiting case, three diamond-shaped pieces will not be covered. Using smaller hexagons will result in other areas being uncovered.

If one looks at a tessellating pattern of hexagons and attempts to circumscribe a hexagon (outer dotted lines), then rectangular-shaped pieces appear. If one attempts to inscribe a hexagon, then six hexagons are cut in half.

FOLLOW-UP REFERENT:
> *When might you need to determine if a given shape will completely cover a surface?*

Examples: installing floor or ceiling tiles, wall paneling, bricks, concrete blocks, siding, roofing; techniques used in highway or building construction; quilting patterns; designing packaging materials; minimizing waste in cutting patterns

CURRICULUM APPLICATION:
Language Arts: ————————
Mathematics: exercises in tessellation; area problems
Science: observing tessellation in biological and physical science, e.g., honeycombs, eye segmentation, crystal growth
Social Studies: estimating relative sizes of geographic areas or features
Enrichment Areas: the art of Maurits Escher; art exercises involving positive and negative space; proportioning art or pictures to fit given areas in newspaper or yearbook layouts

EXTENDING ACTIVITIES:
None.

POLYOMINOES

STRAND: Figural Similarities   **PAGES:** 75–78

ADDITIONAL MATERIALS:
Transparency of student workbook page 75
Transparency of TM #17 (cut apart as indicated)
Student handouts of TM #17
Scissors for students
Washable transparency marker

INTRODUCTION:
> *Some of you have probably played dominoes. A domino is a rectangle made of two touching congruent squares. A group of three touching congruent squares is called a tromino, and a group of multiple touching congruent squares is called a polyomino.*

OBJECTIVE:
> *In these exercises you will use figures composed of groups of polyominoes.*

DEMONSTRATION/EXPLANATION:
Project the transparency of page 75.
> *This shows groupings of congruent squares. The groups are named according to the number of squares in the group. A single square is called a monomino? What is a group of two touching squares called?*

Answer: A domino.

What is a group of three touching squares called?
Answer: A tromino.
What is a group of four touching squares called?
Answer: A tetromino.
What is special about the way the congruent squares are joined?
Possible answers: There is no overlapping; one complete side of each square coincides with one complete side of another square. Indicate the sentence at the top of the page.

"Polyominoes are formed by congruent squares placed next to each other so that their entire sides coincide." Notice that a monomino or a domino can take only one form. How many forms can trominoes take?
Answer: Two; straight line and L-shaped.
How many forms can tetrominoes take?
Answer: Five; straight line, L-shaped, T-shaped, square, and Z-shaped. Distribute handouts of TM #17 and have the students cut out the trominoes.

When you have cut out the trominoes, use them to cover the unshaded rectangular surface.
Project TM #17. Indicate the four cutout trominoes.

These four trominoes are congruent to those on your sheets. Would someone demonstrate how to cover this rectangle using these four trominoes?
Student demonstration.

Is there another tromino pattern that will cover the rectangle?
Student demonstration. Continue optional solutions as time permits or until no further alternatives arise from the students. Possible answers include:

 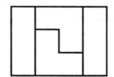 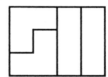 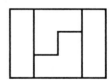

GUIDED PRACTICE:
EXERCISE: **A-190**
Give students sufficient time to complete this exercise. Then, using the demonstration methodology above, have them demonstrate, discuss, and explain their choice.
ANSWER:

A-190

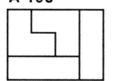 **or** 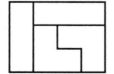   (Or any of the solutions shown for TM #17.)

INDEPENDENT PRACTICE:
Assign exercises **A-191** through **A-194**

DISCUSSION TIPS:
Encourage students to provide as many alternative answers as possible and to produce paper models to test their designs. These exercises make an excellent small-group activity.

ANSWERS:

A-191 (3-pair tetrominoes)

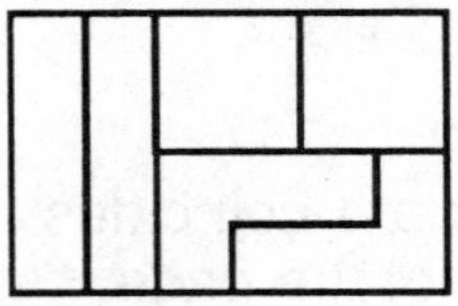

or 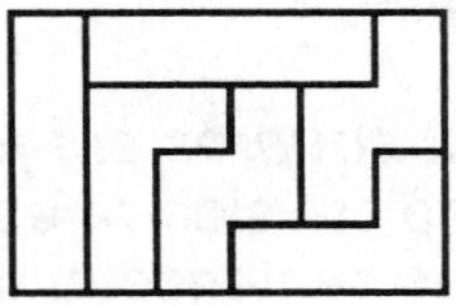   or

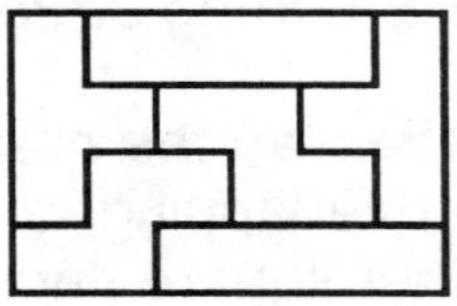

A-192 (3-pair tetrominoes)

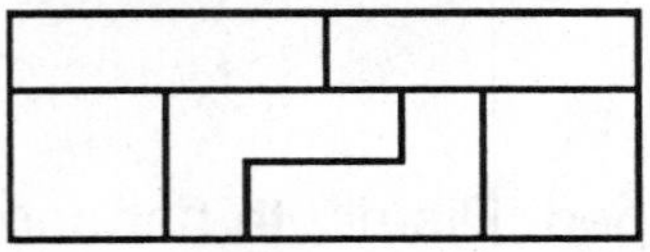

or 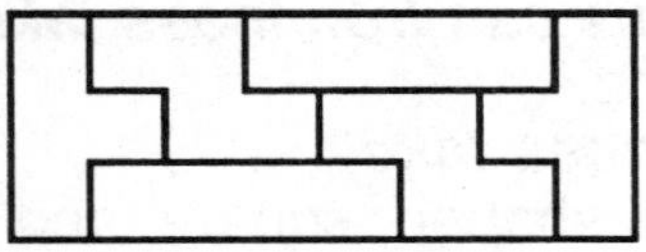   or

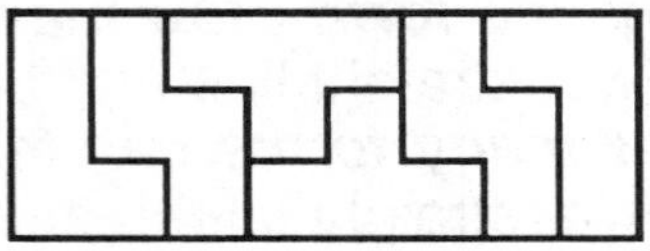

A-193 Twelve pentominoes patterns are shown below. The numbers match those shown in the solution to A-194.

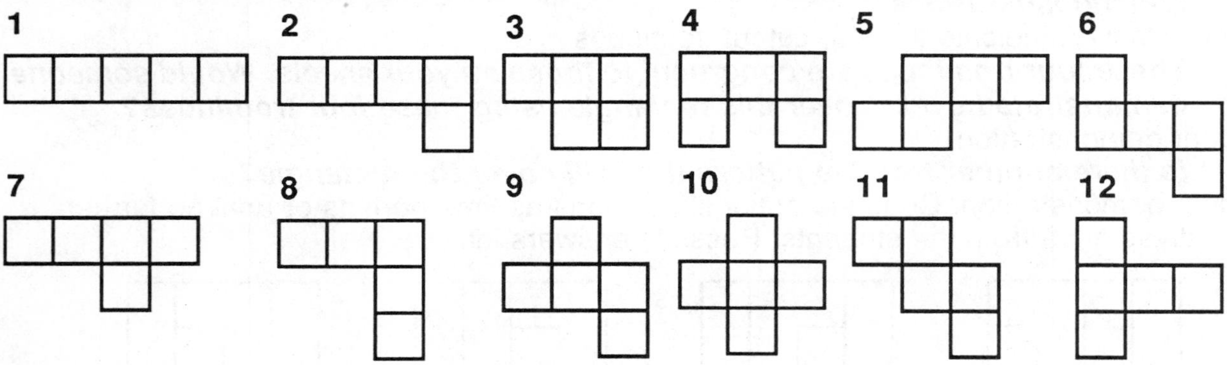

A-194

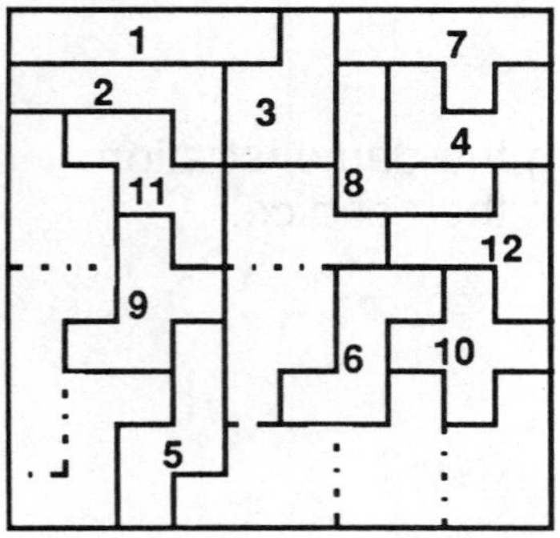

It is possible to use all twelve pentominoes in covering the 10-by-10-unit surface. Here is one possible solution; there are many others.

FOLLOW-UP REFERENT:

When might you need to cover a surface completely with a given group of shapes?

Examples: installing floor or ceiling tiles, wall paneling, bricks, concrete blocks, siding, roofing; techniques used in highway or building construction; quilting patterns; designing packaging materials; minimizing waste in cutting patterns

CURRICULUM APPLICATION:

Language Arts: ——————

Mathematics: tessellation exercises; area problems

Science: observing tessellations in biological and physical science, e.g., honeycombs, eye segmentation, crystal growth
Social Studies: estimating relative sizes of geographic areas or features
Enrichment Areas: the art of Maurits Escher; art exercises involving positive and negative space; proportioning art or pictures to fit given areas in newspaper, magazine, or yearbook layouts

EXTENDING ACTIVITIES:
None.

HOW MANY CUBES MAKE UP THE SOLID?/MATCHING VOLUME

STRAND: Figural Similarities   **PAGES:** 79–82

ADDITIONAL MATERIALS:
Transparencies of student workbook pages 79 and 81
Washable transparency marker

INTRODUCTION:
In previous exercises you worked with flat surfaces only. Now you are going to look at pictures of solids. Since it is impossible to put a solid object on the page of a book, it is necessary to "trick the eye" into thinking it is looking at a solid object.

OBJECTIVE:
In these exercises you will learn to recognize matching groups of cubes.

DEMONSTRATION/EXPLANATION:
Project the transparency of page 79.
These are groupings of identical cubes. In the EXAMPLE you can see two cubes side by side. A "2" is written in the answer blank to indicate the number of cubes.
Indicate the cubes and the numeral.
How many cubes do you see in group a of exercise A-195?
Answer: Two. Write the numeral **2** in the blank provided.
How are they placed?
Answer: Stacked (or one on top of the other).

GUIDED PRACTICE:
EXERCISE: remainder of **A-195**
Give students sufficient time to complete this exercise. Then, using the demonstration methodology above, have them discuss and explain their choices.
ANSWERS: **A-195 b** 2; **c** 3; **d** 3; **e** 3; **f** 4; **g** 4; **h** 4; **i** 5

INDEPENDENT PRACTICE:
Assign exercises **A-196** through **A-205**

DISCUSSION TIPS:
It may be helpful for students to stack wooden blocks or sugar cubes to demonstrate volume relationships.

ANSWERS:
A-196 a 7; **b** 6; **c** 5; **d** 5; **e** 6; **f** 6; **g** 7; **h** 7; **i** 7; **j** 8
A-197 c; **A-198** e; **A-199** b; **A-200** a; **A-201** c; **A-202** a; **A-203** b; **A-204** e; **A-205** d

FOLLOW-UP REFERENT:
> *When might you need to recognize equivalent volume?*

Examples: comparison shopping requiring discriminating between package sizes; estimating storage needs in the home or business; packing for travel; construction games and cube puzzles; designing packaging containers; storing food and liquids; using computer graphics software

CURRICULUM APPLICATION:
Language Arts: —————————
Mathematics: conservation of volume; observing the effect of change or variety of base and height proportions on volume; conceptualizing volume formulas
Science: estimating equivalent volume or storage capacity in laboratory exercises
Social Studies: analyzing building shapes from different cultures
Enrichment Areas: architectural drafting; reading specifications or blueprints in building construction; perception of volume or depth in sculpture

EXTENDING ACTIVITIES:
None.

RECOGNIZING VOLUME

STRAND: Figural Similarities   **PAGES:** 83–85

ADDITIONAL MATERIALS:
Transparency of student workbook page 83
Washable transparency marker

INTRODUCTION:
> *In previous exercises you tessellated shapes into similar figures and counted cubes arranged in different ways.*

OBJECTIVE:
> *In these exercises you will combine these skills. Solids will be stacked into groups similar in shape to the solids being stacked. You will count the number of small solids contained in the similar larger solid.*

DEMONSTRATION/EXPLANATION:
Project the transparency of page 83. Indicate the corresponding solids as you talk.

Exercise A-206 shows a large cube made up of congruent smaller cubes. How many smaller cubes do you see in the top row of the larger cube?

Answer: Four. Write <u>4</u> in the blank.

Assuming that all the cubes you see in the top rows are stacked on other cubes, how many cubes must there be in the bottom rows?

Answer: Four. Write <u>4</u> in the blank.

How many smaller cubes does the larger cube contain?

Answer: Eight. Write <u>8</u> in the blank.

GUIDED PRACTICE:

EXERCISE: **A-207**

Give students sufficient time to complete this exercise. Then, have them discuss and explain their choices.

ANSWER: **A-207** Top <u>4</u>; Bottom <u>4</u>; Total <u>8</u>

INDEPENDENT PRACTICE:

Assign exercises **A-208** through **A-211**

DISCUSSION TIPS:

Some students may generalize that, when one doubles the sides of a solid, the volume is 2 x 2 x 2, or 8 times as great. When one makes the sides of a solid three times as large, then the volume is 3 x 3 x 3, or 27 times as great.

ANSWERS:

A-208 Top <u>9</u>; Middle <u>9</u>; Bottom <u>9</u>; Total <u>27</u>; **A-209** Top <u>9</u>; Middle <u>9</u>; Bottom <u>9</u>; Total <u>27</u>
A-210 Top <u>4</u>; Bottom <u>4</u>; Total <u>8</u>; **A-211** Top <u>9</u>; Middle <u>9</u>; Bottom <u>9</u>; Total <u>27</u>

FOLLOW-UP REFERENT:

When might you need to determine how many smaller solids it would take to make a similar larger solid?

Examples: comparison shopping requiring discriminating between package sizes; estimating storage needs in the home or business; packing for travel; construction games and cube puzzles; designing packaging containers; storing food and liquids; using computer graphics software

CURRICULUM APPLICATION:

Language Arts: ————————

Mathematics: conservation of volume; observing the effect of change or variety of base and height proportions on volume; conceptualizing volume formulas

Science: estimating equivalent volume or storage capacity in laboratory exercises

Social Studies: analyzing building shapes from different cultures

Enrichment Areas: architectural drafting; reading specifications or blueprints in building construction; perception of volume or depth in sculpture; equivalent measures in home economics, or in vocational or industrial arts

EXTENDING ACTIVITIES:

None.

IDENTIFYING AND MATCHING CONGRUENT SOLIDS

STRAND: Figural Similarities   **PAGES:** 86–90

ADDITIONAL MATERIALS:
Transparency of student workbook page 86
Washable transparency marker

INTRODUCTION:
In previous exercises you learned to recognize and compare the size and shape of regular solids. Many solid shapes, however, are not so basic as those with which you have been working.

OBJECTIVE:
In these exercises you will match congruent solids. Congruent solids must have both the same shape and the same volume.

DEMONSTRATION/EXPLANATION:
Project the transparency of page 86.
This EXAMPLE illustrates the procedure you are to follow. The second and fourth solids are congruent and have been circled. They have the same width, the same height, and the same length. If all measurements are the same, then the size and the volume are the same. How does the first solid differ from the second and fourth solids?
Answer: The length of the side is shorter.
Would the volume of the first cube be more or less than that of the two congruent cubes?
Answer: Less.
How do you know?
Answer: The width and depth appear to be about the same, but if the length is shorter, the volume would be less.
How is the third cube different from the two congruent cubes?
Answer: The side is too long.
How does the volume of this cube compare to that of the second or fourth cubes?
Answer: It should be greater, since the width and depth appear to be the same and the length is longer.

GUIDED PRACTICE:
EXERCISES: **A-212, A-213, A-214**
Give students sufficient time to complete these exercises. Then, using the demonstration methodology above, have them discuss and explain their choices.
ANSWERS: **A-212** a and b; **A-213** b and d; **A-214** c and d

INDEPENDENT PRACTICE:
Assign exercises **A-215** through **A-232**

DISCUSSION TIPS:
Have students explain how the nonmatching solids differ from the congruent pair.

Encourage them to use the terms **height**, **width**, **depth**, **volume**, **size**, **congruent**, and **similar** when discussing their answers.

ANSWERS:
A-215 b and c;　**A-216** a and d;　**A-217** b and d;　**A-218** c and d;　**A-219** a and c
A-220 d;　**A-221** b;　**A-222** c;　**A-223** a
A-224 d;　**A-225** c;　**A-226** a;　**A-227** b
A-228 e;　**A-229** d;　**A-230** a;　**A-231** c;　**A-232** b

FOLLOW-UP REFERENT:
　　　When might you need to identify congruent solids?
Examples: packing for travel or storage; cube puzzles; construction games; designing packaging containers; storing food and liquids; using computer graphics software

CURRICULUM APPLICATION:
Language Arts: —————
Mathematics: conceptualizing volume formulas; recognizing congruent solids
Science: estimating volume or storage capacity in laboratory exercises
Social Studies: —————
Enrichment Areas: architectural drafting; reading specifications or blueprints in building
　　construction; perception of volume in sculpture

EXTENDING ACTIVITIES:
None.

RECOGNIZING VIEWS OF A SOLID

STRAND: Figural Similarities　　　　　　　　　**PAGES:** 91–94

ADDITIONAL MATERIALS:
Transparency of student workbook page 91
Washable transparency marker

INTRODUCTION:
　　　*Reproducing a solid object from a pattern or set of plans requires at least three
　　　views of that solid—a front view, a side view, and a top view.*

OBJECTIVE:
　　　In these exercises you will identify the side, front, and top views of a solid.

DEMONSTRATION/EXPLANATION:
Project the transparency of page 91. Indicate the diagram at the top of the page.
　　　*This diagram illustrates that in these exercises the top is represented by T, the side
　　　by S, and the front by F. Look at the solid in the EXAMPLE. What shape is the top?*
Answer: Square.

The only group of pattern pieces shown on the right with a square top-view (T) is group d. Do the front (F) and side (S) views in group d also match the solid?
Answer: Yes; they are both rectangular.
What do the three solids in exercises A-233, A-234, and A-235 have in common?
Answer: They have the same width and length (top view).
How are the three solids different?
Answer: They have different heights.

GUIDED PRACTICE:
EXERCISES: **A-233, A-234, A-235**
Give students sufficient time to complete these exercises. Then, using the demonstration methodology above, have them discuss and explain their choices.
ANSWERS: **A-233** a; **A-234** b; **A-235** c

INDEPENDENT PRACTICE:
Assign exercises **A-236** through **A-249**

DISCUSSION TIPS:
Prepare to use shaded patterns or unfolded boxes to demonstrate how different a pattern piece looks disconnected from the solid. Encourage students to compare volumes of the various solids on each page.

ANSWERS:
A-236 c; **A-237** d; **A-238** a; **A-239** b
A-240 b; **A-241** d; **A-242** e; **A-243** c; **A-244** a
A-245 d; **A-246** e; **A-247** b; **A-248** a; **A-249** c

FOLLOW-UP REFERENT:
When might you need to match a one-dimensional pattern with a solid object or shape?
Examples: comparison shopping requiring discriminating between package sizes; estimating storage needs in the home or business; packing for travel; construction games; cube puzzles; designing packaging containers; storing food and liquids; using computer graphics software; constructing solids for displays or models from paper, wood, plastic, or metal; wrapping gifts or constructing free-form packaging

CURRICULUM APPLICATION:
Language Arts: —————————
Mathematics: observing the effect of varying proportions in base and height on volume; conceptualizing volume formulas; conserving volume
Science: conceptualizing the structure of organisms seen from different views
Social Studies: —————————
Enrichment Areas: architectural drafting; reading specifications or blueprints for building construction; visualizing different views of a sculpture

EXTENDING ACTIVITIES:
None.

COMBINING SOLIDS

STRAND: Figural Similarities   **PAGES:** 95–98

ADDITIONAL MATERIALS:
Transparency of student workbook page 95
Washable transparency marker

INTRODUCTION:
In previous exercises you learned to recognize one-dimensional figures which could be made by combining a given group of shapes. In other exercises you matched pairs of congruent solids.

OBJECTIVE:
In these exercises you will identify which two solid shapes have been stacked to form a given solid figure.

DEMONSTRATION/EXPLANATION:
Project the transparency of page 95. Point to the **EXAMPLE** at the top of the page.
    Look at the EXAMPLE. The solid figure is made by joining a tall thin solid and a shorter solid. Which solid matches the shorter one?
Answer: **d**
    Why is c not the correct answer?
Answer: It is a square cube and is deeper than **d**.
    Which solid is the same as the tall solid?
Answer: **b**
    How can you prove that b matches?
Answer: Measure the long side of each. Use a transparent ruler on the overhead projector or have students measure in their workbooks.

GUIDED PRACTICE:
EXERCISES: **A-250, A-251, A-252**
Give students sufficient time to complete these exercises. Then, using the demonstration methodology above, have them discuss and explain their choices.
ANSWERS: **A-250** a and c; **A-251** a and b; **A–252** c and f

INDEPENDENT PRACTICE:
Assign exercises **A-253** through **A-264**

DISCUSSION TIPS:
Students may use cubes, rectangular blocks, or different sized boxes to demonstrate this concept.

ANSWERS:
A-253 e and c;   **A-254** e and f;   **A-255** a and c;   **A-256** a and b
A-257 e and b;   **A-258** c and f;   **A-259** e and a;   **A-260** f and b
A-261 e and d;   **A-262** f and a;   **A-263** e and a;   **A-264** f and d

FOLLOW-UP REFERENT:
>*When might you need to determine which solids can be combined into a given solid figure or a specific space?*

Examples: comparison shopping requiring discriminating between package sizes; estimating storage needs in the home or business; packing for travel; construction games; cube puzzles; designing packaging containers; storing food and liquids; using computer graphics software

CURRICULUM APPLICATION:
Language Arts: —————
Mathematics: observing the effect of change or variety in proportions of base and height on volume; conceptualizing volume formulas
Science: estimating volume or storage capacity in laboratory exercises
Social Studies: analyzing the shapes of buildings in different cultures
Enrichment Areas: architectural drafting; reading specifications or blueprints in building construction; perceiving volume in sculpture

EXTENDING ACTIVITIES:
None.

COMPLETE THE CUBE WITH ONE PIECE

STRAND: Figural Similarities   **PAGES:** 99–102

ADDITIONAL MATERIALS:
Transparency of student workbook page 99
Washable transparency marker
Transparent ruler (optional)

INTRODUCTION:
>*In previous exercises you chose one shape that would complete a square.*

OBJECTIVE:
>*In these exercises you will find the solid shape that will complete a cube.*

DEMONSTRATION/EXPLANATION:
Project the transparency of page 99. Point to the **EXAMPLE** at the top of the page.
>*In the EXAMPLE, a piece is missing from the cube. Visualize the piece that would make it complete and choose a piece on the right that completes the cube.*

Answer: **a**
>*Why is **b** not correct?*

Answer: It is too wide.
>*Why is **c** not correct?*

Answer: It is too short.
>*Why is **d** not correct?*

Answer: It is too tall.

GUIDED PRACTICE:
EXERCISES: **A-265, A-266**
Give students sufficient time to complete these exercises. Then, using the demonstration methodology above, have them discuss and explain their choices. Use a transparent ruler on the overhead projector to check dimensions if necessary.
ANSWERS: **A-265** b; **A-266** b

INDEPENDENT PRACTICE:
Assign exercises **A-267** through **A-275**

DISCUSSION TIPS:
Help students identify solids in the classroom. Disassemble solids which can be sectioned and allow students to perceive how the solid appears with a portion missing. Encourage students to specify **base**, **height**, and **thickness** when describing why the correct answer fits and the others do not.

ANSWERS:
A-267 c; **A-268** c; **A-269** b; **A-270** c; **A-271** d; **A-272** c; **A-273** b; **A-274** d; **A-275** c

FOLLOW-UP REFERENT:
> *When might you need to choose a piece that will complete a regularly shaped solid?*

Examples: estimating storage needs in the home or business; packing for travel; cube puzzles; construction games; storing food and liquids; using computer graphics software; deciding which model piece or equipment part is missing

CURRICULUM APPLICATION:
Language Arts: —————————
Mathematics: conserving volume; conceptualizing volume formulas Science: estimating volume or storage capacity in laboratory exercises; observing missing or damaged tissue in examination of organisms
Science: estimating volume or storage capacity in laboratory exercises; observing missing or damaged tissue in examination of organisms
Social Studies: ------------
Enrichment Areas: reading blueprints in building construction; volume perception in sculpture construction

EXTENDING ACTIVITIES:
None.

FIGURAL SEQUENCES

SEQUENCE OF FIGURES/SHAPES—SELECT

STRAND: Figural Sequences

PAGES: 103–105

ADDITIONAL MATERIALS:
Transparency of TM #18 (cut apart as indicated)
Transparency of TM #19 (cut apart as indicated)

INTRODUCTION:
Have you ever seen a display showing a series of developing chicken embryos as they appear within the egg? After you have looked closely at several growing embryos, you can almost predict how large and how much more distinct the next embryo will look. You have analyzed the sequence of development.

OBJECTIVE:
This lesson also deals with sequences. In these exercises you will determine what the sequence is by looking at a pattern of changes in a series of figures and recognize the sequence of changes involving appearance or size.

DEMONSTRATION/EXPLANATION:
Project TM #18. Place the cutout figure at the bottom of the screen and point to the first sequence of figures in the top row.
> *Look at the sequence of figures in row 1. Can one of you manipulate the large figure to show how the figures in row 1 change?*

Student demonstration.
> *How would you describe the motion just demonstrated?*

Answer: The pattern is rotating clockwise (to the right).
> *Which figure from the CHOICE BOX should come next?*

Answer: **b**; the black portion should be on the left side.
> *Look at the sequence in row 2. Can one of you manipulate the large figure to show how the figures in row 2 change?*

Student demonstration.
> *How would you describe the motion just demonstrated?*

Answer: The pattern is rotating counterclockwise (to the left).
> *Which figure from the CHOICE BOX should come next?*

Answer: **d**; the black portion should be on the right side.
> *Look at the sequence in row 3. Can one of you manipulate the large figure to show how these figures change?*

Student demonstration.
> *How would you describe the motion just demonstrated?*

Answer: The pattern is reflecting about the vertical axis (flipping back and forth). The black part stays on top and the shaded and white parts exchange positions: white right, white left, white right.
> *Which figure from the CHOICE BOX should come next?*

Answer: **a**; the black portion should stay on top and the white part should be on the left.
> *Look at the sequence again. As the white part moves from right to left, what line stays in place?*

Answer: One of the vertical side lines stays in the same place. (You can reflect about either the left or right side.) Place a straw or pencil along a side vertical and flip the large pattern about it.
> *This is known as reflection* (flipping) *about a vertical line. Look at the sequence in row 4. Can one of you manipulate the large figure to show the changes in this sequence?*

Student demonstration.
> *How would you describe the motion just demonstrated?*

Answer: The black part reflects from top to bottom and the shaded and white parts stay on the left and right. The pattern is reflecting top to bottom.
> *Which figure from the CHOICE BOX should come next?*

Answer: **c**; the black portion should reflect to the bottom and the white part should be on the right.
> *Look at the reflection again. As the large shaded part moves from top to bottom, what line stays in place?*

Answer: One horizontal line stays in the same place. Place a straw or pencil along a horizontal and reflect the large pattern about it.
> *This is known as reflection* (flipping) *about a horizontal line. So far you have tried two kinds of sequences:* REFLECTIONS *(flips) and* ROTATIONS *(turns).*

Write REFLECTIONS and ROTATIONS on the chalkboard.
> *What is the difference between reflections and rotations? If a figure reflects* (flips), *one side stays in position and the other sides move over or up. You have to pick up one side of the figure and turn it over.*

Flip the square back and forth several times.
> *It can be reflected left and right...*

Flip twice about the vertical axis.
> *...or it can be reflected up and down...*

Flip twice about the horizontal axis.
> *...but each time one side has to be moved through space.*

Pick it up and put it down.
> *In a rotation sequence, you don't have to pick up the figure. You can rotate it clockwise* (to the right)...

Turn the large square to the right four positions.
> *...or you can rotate it counterclockwise* (to the left).

Turn the large square to the left four positions.
> *Either way, the figure remains flat on the surface. You do not have to pick up any part of it.*

Project figure **1** from TM #19.
> *Other sequential patterns may be formed by adding or subtracting details. In this figure, only a bar across the bottom is black.*

Place figure **2** directly over figure **1**.
> *Now the black part has grown to about half the size of the figure.*

Place figure **3** directly over figures **1** and **2**.
> *In this figure, the black part covers most of the square.*

Place figure **4** directly over the first three figures.
>   *Now the entire square is black. This sequence is known as* **ADDING DETAIL.**

Write <u>ADDING DETAIL</u> on the chalkboard.
>   *The reverse process is called* **SUBTRACTING DETAIL.** *This is done in much the same way as you subtract numbers.*

Write <u>SUBTRACTING DETAIL</u> on the chalkboard.
>   *This kind of sequence starts with a lot of color or lines and each time has less. Let's use this figure as an example. At the beginning, the whole square is black.*

Remove figure **4.**
>   *Some of the black space has been subtracted.*

Remove figure **3.**
>   *Now more of the color has been removed, leaving only half of the square black.*

Remove figure **2.**
>   *Now only the bar at the bottom remains. An amount of black space has been subtracted each time. Detail has been removed. The detail in this example is the amount of black space.*

NOTE: *You may have a student who, recognizing the difference between positive and negative space, perceives that in the first demonstration you were "subtracting white" and in the second you were "adding white." That perception is also correct.*
>   ***Look at the EXAMPLE at the top of page 103. What kind of sequence is this?***

Indicate the types of sequences listed on the chalkboard. Answer: clockwise rotation. Ask students to explain why each of the other responses in the **CHOICE BOX** does not fit.

GUIDED PRACTICE:
EXERCISES: **B-1, B-2, B-3, B-4**
Give students sufficient time to complete these exercises. Then, using the demonstration methodology above, have them discuss and explain their choices.
ANSWERS: **B-1** e (adding detail clockwise); **B-2** a (repeating pattern or reflection about the horizontal axis); **B-3** b (rotation counterclockwise); **B-4** d (subtracting detail counterclockwise)

INDEPENDENT PRACTICE:
Assign exercises **B-5** through **B-15**

DISCUSSION TIPS:
Words and phrases students need to know are: **repeating, flip, sequence, horizontal, vertical,** and **axis.** The proper term for "flipping" is **reflection.** Encourage students to use these words in describing sequences. Remember the importance of discussing each exercise.

ANSWERS:
B-5 f; **B-6** c; **B-7** d; **B-8** a; **B-9** e; **B-10** c; **B-11** e; **B-12** a; **B-13** g; **B-14** h; **B-15** b

FOLLOW-UP REFERENT:
>   *Where have you seen repeating patterns of shapes?*

Examples: fabric; brick or concrete block walls; floor or ceiling tiles; Venetian blinds; leaf arrangements on plants; beadings; sequences of letters or numbers; model building

When do you remember having to determine whether something has been flipped?
Examples: when a letter has been reversed; seeing a sign in a mirror, e.g., AMBULANCE in a rearview mirror; handling dress patterns which have to be reflected to cut the second piece; printmaking; photography
When might you need to recognize that something has been rotated?
Examples: art activities; puzzle pieces; reading a map
When might you find it necessary to predict how something will look after details have been added?
Examples: art projects; model building; computer graphics; sewing
When might you need to predict how something will look when details have been removed?
Examples: looking for basic shapes in pictures, scenes, or designs

CURRICULUM APPLICATION:

Language Arts: repeating patterns can be seen in decoding unfamiliar words and when recognizing alliteration and rhyme schemes; rotation is important in letter discrimination abilities and layout or design techniques for journalism projects; adding and subtracting detail is used to form new words by adding or subtracting prefixes and suffixes

Mathematics: repeating patterns can be used as a memorization technique for mathematics tables; reflections can be used to illustrate the associative and commutative rules and is a common concept in elementary school geometry; rotations are used in different arrangements for basic problems, e.g., horizontal or vertical formats and in recognizing geometric position or pattern changes; adding and subtracting detail is used in making charts and graphs

Science: repeating patterns are shown in leaves, shells, and life cycles; reflections can be used to show symmetry in plants and in light reflection exercises, e.g., using a microscope or telescope; rotations can be shown by the rotation of the earth on its axis, e.g., explaining day and night on earth, and when using kaleidoscopes; adding or subtracting detail can be seen in the evolution of different species, making measurements, and model building

Social Studies: repeating patterns are used to show geographic changes or similarities on maps; reflections can be seen when using or making graphs that show positive and negative changes; adding and subtracting detail can be illustrated by comparing different types of maps that show the same geographic area

Enrichment Areas: art exercises involving rotation, reflection, or positive and negative space; repeating time intervals or phrases in music; flipping pattern pieces in sewing or woodworking to produce symmetrical products; creating color charts by combining colors to create new colors or shades; playing games that call for taking turns or doing rotations, e.g., musical chairs or relay races; drafting and architectural drawing; following directions in setting up a tent or constructing a cardboard-carpentry project

EXTENDING ACTIVITIES:
None.

SEQUENCE OF FIGURES—SUPPLY SHADING

STRAND: Figural Sequences   **PAGES:** 106–108

ADDITIONAL MATERIALS:
Transparency of student workbook page 106
Washable transparency marker

INTRODUCTION:
> *In the previous lesson you chose a figure that continued a sequence and learned to recognize several types of sequences: <u>reflections</u>, <u>rotations</u>, <u>adding detail</u>, and <u>subtracting detail</u>.*

Write list of sequence types on the chalkboard.

OBJECTIVE:
> *In these exercises you will shade figures to make them continue a sequence.*

DEMONSTRATION/EXPLANATION:
Project exercise **B-16** from the transparency of page 106.
> *What kind of sequence is this?*

Refer to list on the chalkboard. Answer: Counterclockwise rotation.
> *What must be done to make the next figure continue this sequence?*

Answer: Rotate the previous figure one-quarter turn to the left:

GUIDED PRACTICE:
EXERCISES: **B-17, B-18**
Give students sufficient time to complete these exercises. Then, using the demonstration methodology above, have them discuss and explain their choices.
ANSWERS:

B-17   **B-18**

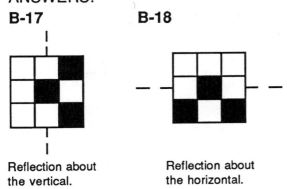

Reflection about   Reflection about
the vertical.   the horizontal.

INDEPENDENT PRACTICE:
Assign exercises **B-19** through **B-30**

DISCUSSION TIPS:
Words and phrases students need to know and use are: **hexagon**, **add detail**, **increase size**, **decrease size**, and **rotate**. Students should always name the sequence and describe how they changed the figure to complete the sequence. *NOTE: Alternate answers may be possible.*

ANSWERS:

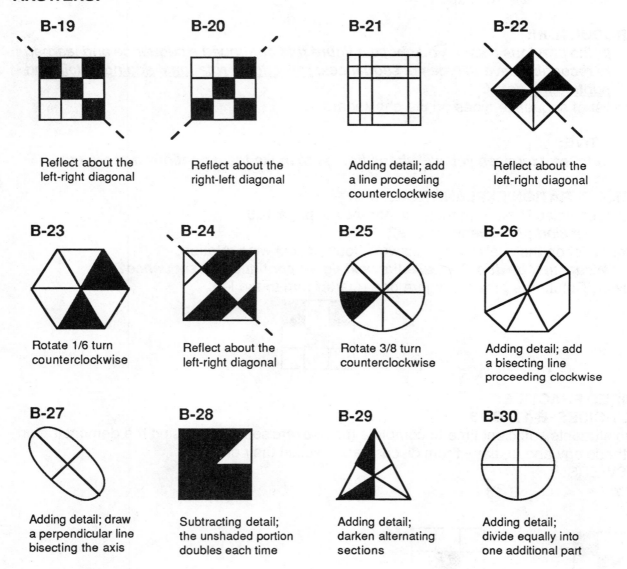

B-19
Reflect about the left-right diagonal

B-20
Reflect about the right-left diagonal

B-21
Adding detail; add a line proceeding counterclockwise

B-22
Reflect about the left-right diagonal

B-23
Rotate 1/6 turn counterclockwise

B-24
Reflect about the left-right diagonal

B-25
Rotate 3/8 turn counterclockwise

B-26
Adding detail; add a bisecting line proceeding clockwise

B-27
Adding detail; draw a perpendicular line bisecting the axis

B-28
Subtracting detail; the unshaded portion doubles each time

B-29
Adding detail; darken alternating sections

B-30
Adding detail; divide equally into one additional part

FOLLOW-UP REFERENT:
When might you need to recognize a sequence and produce the pattern that would come next?
Examples: knitting; weaving; art activities; construction projects

CURRICULUM APPLICATION:
Language Arts: choosing the right word to fill in a rhyme scheme; finding or drawing the right picture to continue or complete a story sequence or a comic strip

Mathematics: filling in missing items of a sequence, e.g., numerals or shapes; completing a mathematical table

Science: recognizing or predicting physiological changes in developmental stages of plants or animals; drawing conclusions or hypotheses from experiments; duplicating experiments

Social Studies: reading and interpreting maps, graphs, or charts

Enrichment Areas: constructing repeated patterns in art projects; memorizing sports, music, or dance patterns

EXTENDING ACTIVITIES:
None.

SEQUENCE OF SHAPES/FIGURES—SUPPLY

STRAND: Figural Sequences   **PAGE:** 109

ADDITIONAL MATERIALS:
Transparency of TM #20
Washable transparency marker

INTRODUCTION:
In the previous exercises you shaded a figure to correctly continue a sequence and worked with several types of sequences: <u>rotations</u>, <u>reflections</u>, <u>adding detail</u>, and <u>subtracting detail</u>.

Write list of sequence types on the chalkboard.

OBJECTIVE:
In these exercises you will continue a sequence by producing (drawing) the next shape or figure.

DEMONSTRATION/EXPLANATION:
Project the top section of TM #20.
What is happening to these diamonds as the sequence proceeds?
Answer: Less of each figure is shaded (all shaded, 3/4 shaded, 1/2 shaded).
What type of sequence is this?
Refer to list on the chalkboard. Answer: Subtracting detail.
How should the last figure be shaded to show a continuing sequence?
Answer: Only the top left quarter of the diamond should be shaded.

Project the bottom section of TM #20.
What do all of these shapes have in common?

89

Answer: They are all circles.
> **What pattern do you see?**

Answer: The circles are getting larger.
> **What kind of a circle comes next?**

Answer: One larger than the last circle.
> **If you call the space between two dots a block, the first circle appears to be about two blocks wide.**

Point with a pencil as you count.
> **The second one appears to be about three blocks wide.**

Point with a pencil as you count.
> **The third one appears to be about four blocks wide.**

Point with a pencil as you count.
> **Use the dot grid as a guide to draw a circle larger than the last one. The circles seem to be changing by adding one block each time, so you would make the next circle five blocks wide in each direction. Mark the extreme points of the circle on the grid, then estimate a curve in between them...**

Draw as you explain.
> **...to make a circle. You don't have to be exact; just estimate the size you want the next figure to be.**

GUIDED PRACTICE:

EXERCISES: **B-31, B-32, B-33**

Give students sufficient time to complete these exercises. Then, using the methodology demonstrated above, have them discuss and explain their choices.

ANSWERS:

B-31

The pattern is wider by one unit, then taller by one unit. The next shape should be three units wide and four units tall.

B-32

The pattern is closed polygons with a decreasing number of sides. The next shape should have four sides.

B-33

The pattern is narrower by one unit, then shorter by one unit. The next shape should be two units wide and three units tall.

INDEPENDENT PRACTICE:

Assign exercises **B-34** and **B-35**

DISCUSSION TIPS:

Words and phrases students need to know and use are: **hexagon**, **add detail**, **increase size**, **decrease size**, and **rotate**. Encourage the students to describe how they changed each shape to complete the sequence.

ANSWERS:

B-34

B-35

The pattern doubles the number of squares, alternating rectangular and square shapes. The next figure should be a square, four units by four units.

The pattern divides the circle into an increasing number of equal parts. The next figure will be divided into six equal parts

FOLLOW-UP REFERENT:

When might you have to identify a pattern and provide the next step?
Examples: knitting; carving; weaving; art activities

CURRICULUM APPLICATION:

Language Arts: choosing the right word to fill in a rhyme scheme; finding or drawing the right picture to continue or complete a story sequence or comic strip

Mathematics: filling in the missing items of a sequence, e.g., numerals or shapes; completing a mathematical table

Science: recognizing or predicting physiological changes in developmental stages of plants or animals; drawing conclusions or hypotheses from experiments; duplicating experiments

Social Studies: reading and interpreting graphs representing election results or legislative procedures; reading and interpreting maps

Enrichment Areas: constructing repeated patterns in art projects; memorizing sports, music, or dance patterns

EXTENDING ACTIVITIES:

None.

SEQUENCE OF SHAPES—SUPPLY

STRAND: Figural Sequences   **PAGES:** 110–112

ADDITIONAL MATERIALS:

Transparency of TM #21
Transparency of student workbook page 110

INTRODUCTION:

In recent exercises you produced or shaded a single drawing to continue a sequence.

OBJECTIVE:
In these exercises you will supply a series of shapes to continue a sequence.

DEMONSTRATION/EXPLANATION:
Project the first two rows from TM #21.
  What do you notice about the shapes in these two rows?
Answer: Each row contains the same shapes, but they are in a different order.
  In these exercises a shape or a group of shapes is picked up and moved to a new location. How might the shapes in the first row have been rearranged to produce the second row?
Allow time for discussion. Answer: The pentagon may have been moved from the right end (back) to the left end (front).
  If your observation is correct, how should the next row look?
Answer: The right triangle should move from the right end to the left end. Expose the third row to verify the answer.
  How should the last row look if the sequence continues?
Answer: The trapezoid should move from the back to the front.

Project the first two rows of the EXAMPLE from the transparency of page 110.
  What do you notice about the shapes in these two rows?
Answer: The shapes are the same, but in a different order.
  How has the first row been changed to produce the second?
Answer: The triangle has been moved from the left end to the right end.
  Can you predict the sequence of shapes in the third row by looking at these rows?
  If your prediction is correct, how should the shapes be arranged in the third row?
Answer: The parallelogram should move from the left end to the right end. Expose the third row to verify the answer.
  How should the last row look when it is drawn in?
Answer: The pentagon should move from the left end to the right end. Project the answer.

GUIDED PRACTICE:
EXERCISE: **B-36**
Give students sufficient time to complete this exercise. Then, using the demonstration methodology above, have them discuss and explain their choice.
ANSWER:

B-36

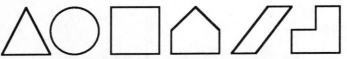
The two shapes from the right end move to the left end.

INDEPENDENT PRACTICE:
Assign exercises **B-37** through **B-40**

DISCUSSION TIPS:
Words and phrases students need to know and use are: **hexagon**, **parallelagram**, and **pentagon**. Students should always name the sequence and describe how they changed the location of the shapes to complete the sequence.

ANSWERS:
B-37

The two shapes from the left end move to the right end.

B-38

The three shapes from the right end move to the left end.

B-39

The three shapes from the right end move to the left end.

B-40

The three shapes from the left end move to the right end.

FOLLOW-UP REFERENT:
When might you need to recognize the pattern within a series and provide the next step?
Examples: knitting; carving; weaving; art activities

CURRICULUM APPLICATION:
Language Arts: choosing the right word to fill in a rhyme scheme; finding or drawing the right picture to continue or complete a story sequence or comic strip
Mathematics: filling in the missing items of a sequence, e.g., numerals or shapes; completing a mathematical table
Science: recognizing or predicting changes in physiological development stages of plants or animals; drawing conclusions or hypotheses from experiments; duplicating experiments
Social Studies: interpreting graphs of election results or legislative procedures; reading and interpreting maps

Enrichment Areas: constructing repeated patterns in art projects; memorizing sports, music, or dance patterns

EXTENDING ACTIVITIES:
None.

ROTATING FIGURES—FIND THE EXCEPTION

STRAND: Figural Sequences   **PAGES:** 113–114

ADDITIONAL MATERIALS:
Transparency of TM #22
Wooden puzzle (optional)

INTRODUCTION:
When you put a puzzle together, sometimes you have to turn pieces to make them fit.
Project TM #22 or several interlocking pieces from a wooden puzzle to demonstrate how the pieces of a puzzle must be turned to fit.

OBJECTIVE:
In these exercises you will estimate how a figure will look after it has been rotated and eliminate any figure that cannot be produced by rotating the given figure.

DEMONSTRATION/EXPLANATION:
Project figure **A** from the top section of TM #22, then rotate it one position clockwise.
This is how the pattern looks when it is rotated one position clockwise.
Return pattern to original position, then rotate it two positions clockwise.
This is how the pattern looks when it is rotated two positions clockwise.
Return pattern to original position, then rotate it three positions clockwise.
This is how the pattern looks when it is rotated three positions clockwise. Look at the EXAMPLE on page 113. How many positions is the original figure rotated to produce figure a?
Answer: One position.
How many positions is the original figure rotated in figure c?
Answer: Two.
What rotation produced figure d?
Answer: Three.
Why has figure b been crossed out?
Answer: It cannot be produced by rotating the original figure.
Could you produce figure b from the original figure?
Answer: Yes, by reversing the colors, then rotating it one position clockwise. Project figure **B** from TM #22 (**B-41**).
This figure is the same as the original figure shown in exercise B-41.
Rotate the figure one position clockwise.

This is how the pattern looks when it is rotated one position clockwise. Is this one of the possible answers shown for this exercise?

Answer: No. Return pattern to its original position, then rotate it two positions clockwise.

This is how the pattern looks when it is rotated two positions clockwise. Is this one of the answer choices?

Answer: Yes, **b**. Return pattern to its original position, then rotate it three positions clockwise.

This is how the pattern looks when it is rotated three positions clockwise. Is this one of the answer choices?

Answer: Yes, **a** and **d**.

Which of the answer figures cannot be produced by rotating this pattern?

Answer: **c**.

Could you form figure c using the original figure?

Answer: Yes, by rotating the figure three positions clockwise (or one counterclockwise) and reflecting it about a vertical axis. Demonstrate the movements to confirm the answer.

GUIDED PRACTICE:
EXERCISES: **B-42, B-43, B-44**
Give students sufficient time to complete these exercises. Then, using the demonstration methodology above, have them discuss and explain their choices. If possible, have them explain how the eliminated figure might be created from the original.
ANSWERS: **B-42** d; **B-43** c; **B-44** a

INDEPENDENT PRACTICE:
Assign exercises **B-45** through **B-49**

DISCUSSION TIPS:
The key word in this exercise is **rotation**. Ask students to identify school objects or sports movements that illustrate this term. The rotating surface of a phonograph turntable is a helpful association.

ANSWERS:
B-45 c; **B-46** b; **B-47** d; **B-48** a; **B-49** b

FOLLOW-UP REFERENT:
When might you need to predict how a pattern will look when it has been rotated?
Examples: puzzle pieces; reading a map; assembling models or dress patterns

CURRICULUM APPLICATION:
Language Arts: distinguishing between vertical and horizontal design in journalism
Mathematics: rotating geometric shapes; reversing mathematic processes as an accuracy check; adding or subtracting multiple columns of figures in a horizontal format
Science: explaining rotation of the earth, the solar system, lunar and solar eclipses; experiments using mirrors or gears
Social Studies: map reading skills involving longitude and latitude; map orientation; redrawing charts or graphs into other forms

Enrichment Areas: career education discussions involving architecture, engineering, construction, drafting, graphic design, dental practice, radiology, archaeology; folk or square dancing patterns; quilting or needlework pattern repetitions

EXTENDING ACTIVITIES:
None.

ROTATING SHAPES—SUPPLY

STRAND: Figural Sequences   **PAGES:** 115–116

ADDITIONAL MATERIALS:
Transparency of TM #23 (cut apart as indicated)
Large cardboard squares

INTRODUCTION:
In the previous exercise you observed how a figure looks when it has been rotated to different positions.

OBJECTIVE:
In these exercises you will draw a shape as it should look after it has been rotated.

DEMONSTRATION/EXPLANATION:
Optional lesson plans:
Option 1: Use chalk to draw large shapes on cardboard squares. Use the chalk rail or a yardstick as a track for rotation as you demonstrate the following activity.
Option 2: Project the two shapes within the squares cut from the top section of TM #23.
You are to predict how a shape drawn on a square will look after it has been turned one or more positions so it comes to rest again on another flat side. Here is a four-sided shape like the EXAMPLE on page 115. Watch what happens as it rotates.
Turn the quadrilateral clockwise slowly as you talk so students can see what "coming to rest" means.
The quadrilateral starts at rest, turns clockwise (to the right) one position (to the next edge), and comes to rest again.
On the chalkboard, draw a curved arrow to the right and label it <u>CLOCKWISE</u>. Return the quadrilateral to its original position.
Objects can also rotate counterclockwise (to the left).
Demonstrate as you talk.
The shape begins at rest, turns counterclockwise (to the left) one position (to the next edge), and comes to rest again.
On the chalkboard, draw a curved arrow to the left and label it <u>COUNTERCLOCKWISE</u>.

GUIDED PRACTICE:
EXERCISES: **B-50, B-51, B-52**
Give students sufficient time to complete these exercises. Then, using the demonstration methodology above, have them discuss and explain their choices. *NOTE:* TM #23

contains a shape like **B-50** *to use for demonstration or verification. If necessary, you may trace the shapes in* **B-51** *and* **B-52** *on a transparency.*

ANSWERS: Students are to supply the underlined shapes.

B-50

B-51

B-52

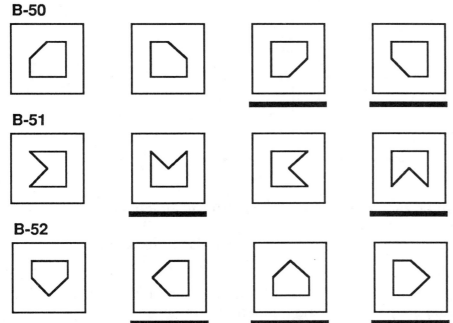

INDEPENDENT PRACTICE:
Assign exercises **B-53** through **B-56**

DISCUSSION TIPS:
Key words in this exercise are **clockwise**, **counterclockwise**, and **rotation**. Have students use these terms in discussing the solutions. Ask students to identify objects in school or movements in sports that use these terms. The rotation of a phonograph turntable may be a helpful association.

ANSWERS: Students are to supply the underlined patterns.

B-53

B-54

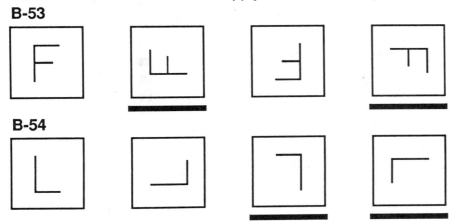

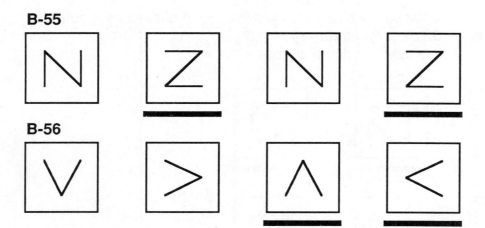

B-55

B-56

FOLLOW-UP REFERENT:
When might you need to predict how a shape or pattern will look after it has been rotated?
Examples: puzzle pieces; reading a map; putting together models or dress patterns

CURRICULUM APPLICATION:
Language Arts: distinguishing between vertical and horizontal design in journalism
Mathematics: rotating geometric shapes; reversing mathematic processes as an
    accuracy check; adding or subtracting multiple columns of figures in a horizontal format
Science: explaining rotation of the earth, the solar system, lunar and solar eclipses;
    experiments using mirrors or gears
Social Studies: map reading skills involving longitude and latitude; map orientation;
    redrawing charts or graphs
Enrichment Areas: career education discussions involving architecture, engineering,
    construction, drafting, graphic design, dental practice, radiology, archaeology; folk or
    square dancing patterns; quilting or needlework pattern repetitions; rotating positions
    in sports, especially volleyball

EXTENDING ACTIVITIES:
None.

ROTATING FIGURES—SUPPLY

STRAND: Figural Sequences   **PAGE:** 117

ADDITIONAL MATERIALS:
Transparency of TM #23 (cut apart as indicated)
Large triangle, square, and hexagon attribute blocks (or shapes cut from cardboard)

INTRODUCTION
*In the previous exercises you predicted positions and drew a shape or pattern
inside a square as it rotated through various positions.*

OBJECTIVE:

In these exercises you will estimate how a more complex figure will look after it has been rotated a certain number of positions in a given direction.

DEMONSTRATION/EXPLANATION:

Optional lesson plans:

Option 1: Number the corners of the large cardboard or attribute block shapes with chalk. Use the chalk rail or a yardstick as a track for the demonstration.

Option 2: Cut out the figures from TM #23. Project the square-shape (**EXAMPLE**, page 118), turning it slowly so students can see what "coming to rest" means.

You are to predict where the inside shapes will be located as the square is rotated through one or more positions so it comes to rest again on another flat side.

Turn the figure clockwise as you talk so students can see what "coming to rest" means.

The figure starts at rest, turns clockwise (to the right) *one position* (to the next side), *and comes to rest again.*

On the chalkboard, draw a curved arrow to the right and label it CLOCKWISE. Return the square to its original position.

Objects can also rotate counterclockwise (to the left).

Demonstrate as you talk.

The figure begins at rest, turns counterclockwise (to the left) *one position* (to the next side), *and comes to rest again.*

On the chalkboard, draw a curved arrow to the left and label it COUNTERCLOCKWISE. Return the figure to its original position and indicate the circle in the lower left corner.

Where will the small circle be located if the square is rotated two positions clockwise?

Allow time for student discussion,

Where will the triangle be located?

Allow time for discussion, then demonstrate the rotation to confirm the answer. Ask students to be specific in their statements of location. Return the figure to its original position and repeat the process with different positions and directions. Demonstrate other rotations using the square and hexagon shapes.

GUIDED PRACTICE:

EXERCISES: **B-57, B-58**

Give students sufficient time to complete these exercises. Then, using the demonstration methodology above, have them discuss and explain their choices.

ANSWERS:

B-57   **B-58**

INDEPENDENT PRACTICE:

Assign exercises **B-59** and **B-60**

DISCUSSION TIPS:

Key words in this exercise are **clockwise**, **counterclockwise**, and **rotation**. Students should always state the direction of the rotation (clockwise or counterclockwise). Ask students to identify objects in school or movements in sports using these terms. A helpful association is the rotating surface of a phonograph turntable.

ANSWERS:

B-59   **B-60**

FOLLOW-UP REFERENT:

When might you need to predict how a figure or pattern will look after it has been rotated?

Examples: puzzle pieces; reading a map; assembling models or dress patterns

CURRICULUM APPLICATION:

Language Arts: distinguishing between vertical and horizontal design in journalism

Mathematics: rotating geometric shapes; reversing mathematic processes as an accuracy check; adding or subtracting multiple columns of figures in a horizontal format

Science: explaining rotation of the earth, the solar system, lunar and solar eclipses; experiments using mirrors or gears

Social Studies: map reading skills involving longitude and latitude; map orientation; redrawing charts or graphs

Enrichment Areas: career education discussions involving architecture, engineering, construction, drafting, graphic design, dental practice, radiology, archaeology; folk or square dancing patterns; quilting or needlework pattern repetitions; rotated patterns or positions in sports plays, especially volleyball

EXTENDING ACTIVITIES:

None.

ROTATING FIGURES—EXPLAIN

STRAND: Figural Sequences   **PAGES:** 118–119

ADDITIONAL MATERIALS:

Transparency of TM #23 (cut apart as indicated)
Large triangle, square, and hexagon attribute blocks (or shapes cut from cardboard)

INTRODUCTION

In the previous exercise you predicted how figures would look after they had been rotated.

OBJECTIVE:

In these exercises you will be given two views of a figure and asked to determine the direction of the rotation and the number of turns necessary to produce the second view of the figure.

DEMONSTRATION/EXPLANATION:

Optional lesson plans:

Option 1: Use chalk to mark a large cardboard or attribute square as shown in the **EXAMPLE** on student workbook page 118. Use the chalk rail or a yardstick as a track.

Option 2: Project the square from TM #23 (**EXAMPLE**, page 118) in its original position.

> *This is position a…*

Turn the square slowly one position to the right.

> *…and this is position b. How was the square rotated to change it from a to b?*

Answer: One position clockwise (to the right).

> *Is it possible to rotate the square counterclockwise and change it from position a to position b?*

Answer: Yes; three positions counterclockwise (to the left). Demonstrate the rotation.

> *Thus there are two possible correct answers:*
> *1. Turn the square one position clockwise (to the right).*
> *2. Turn the square three positions counterclockwise (to the left).*

Demonstrate similar rotations using the triangle and hexagons. An alert student may comment that there are many solutions; actually $(1 + 4n)$ to the right equals $(3 + 4n)$ to the left, where $n = 1, 2, 3, 4, 5....$

GUIDED PRACTICE:

EXERCISE: **B-61**

Give students sufficient time to complete this exercise. Then, using the demonstration methodology above, have them discuss and explain their choice.

ANSWER: **B-61** The square has been rotated one position counterclockwise (or three positions clockwise).

INDEPENDENT PRACTICE:

Assign exercises **B-62** and **B-69**

DISCUSSION TIPS:

Key words in this exercise are **clockwise, counterclockwise**, and **rotation**. Students should always state the direction in which the figure was rotated (counterclockwise or clockwise) and the number of turns. Ask students to identify objects in school or movements in sports using these terms. A helpful association is the rotating surface of a phonograph turntable.

ANSWERS:

B-62 The hexagon has been rotated two positions counterclockwise (or four positions clockwise);

B-63 The hexagon has been rotated three positions counterclockwise (or three positions clockwise);

B-64 The hexagon has been rotated five positions counterclockwise (or one position clockwise);

B-65 The triangle has been rotated two positions counterclockwise (or one position clockwise);

B-66 The square has been rotated two positions counterclockwise (or two positions clockwise);

B-67 The triangle has been rotated one position counterclockwise (or two positions clockwise);

B-68 The hexagon has been rotated four positions counterclockwise (or two positions clockwise);

B-69 The hexagon has been rotated two positions counterclockwise (or four positions clockwise)

FOLLOW-UP REFERENT:
When might you need to explain how a shape or pattern was rotated?
Examples: telling someone how to turn puzzle pieces, a map, or a pattern

CURRICULUM APPLICATION:
Language Arts: distinguishing between vertical and horizontal design in journalism
Mathematics: rotating geometric shapes; reversing mathematic processes as an accuracy check; adding or subtracting multiple columns of figures in a horizontal format
Science: explaining rotation of the earth, the solar system, lunar and solar eclipses; experiments using mirrors or gears
Social Studies: map reading skills involving longitude and latitude; map orientation; redrawing charts or graphs
Enrichment Areas: career education discussions involving architecture, construction, drafting, graphic design, archaeology, or engineering; recognizing and explaining folk or square dancing patterns; describing quilting or needlework pattern repetitions

EXTENDING ACTIVITIES:
None.

PRODUCING SINGLE REFLECTIONS

STRAND: Figural Sequences   **PAGES:** 120–121

ADDITIONAL MATERIALS:
Transparency of TM #24
Washable transparency marker

INTRODUCTION:
When you look in a mirror you see a reflection of yourself in reverse.

OBJECTIVE:
In these exercises you will shade figures to show a given type of reflection. You will practice three types of reflections: vertical, horizontal, and diagonal.

DEMONSTRATION/EXPLANATION:

Project figure **A** (EXAMPLE, student workbook page 120) from TM #24.

> ***You are to shade a figure as it will look after it has been reflected about a given axis (line). Try to visualize how this pattern will look when it has been reflected about a vertical axis.***

Allow time for student discussion, reflect the transparency pattern about the vertical axis as shown in the **EXAMPLE** on page 120, then return it to the original position.

> ***Notice how the figure changes. The parts that were on the top and bottom of the original figure are still on the top and bottom...***

Reflect the pattern piece about the vertical again to confirm this statement, then return to original position.

> ***...but the part that was to the left of the vertical axis is now to the right and the part that was to the right is now to the left.***

Demonstrate the reflection again, returning the figure to the original position.

> ***A reflection about the vertical axis is indicated in these exercises by a vertical dotted line through the center of the figure.***

Draw a dotted vertical line on the transparency figure, reflect the figure, return it to the original position, and remove the line.

> ***A second type of reflection is about the horizontal axis.***

Draw a dotted horizontal line through the center of the figure.

> ***Try to visualize how this figure will look after it has been reflected about this line. How will a horizontal reflection change the figure?***

Answer: The part that is above the axis will be below and the part that is below will be above. Reflect the transparency figure about the horizontal to confirm student answers.

> ***Notice the shading that was to the right remains to the right and what was to the left remains to the left.***

Repeat the horizontal reflection several times with the transparency figure. Remove figure **A** from the projector and project figure **B**.

> ***The third type of reflection is about a diagonal axis. Diagonal axes can go two directions: from top left to bottom right...***

Indicate the mentioned corners on the figure.

> ***...or from top right to bottom left.***

Indicate the corners.

> ***Again, the axis of reflection is indicated by a dotted line.***

Draw a left-right diagonal dotted line through the center of the figure.

> ***Can you visualize this figure after it has been reflected about this diagonal?***

Allow time for student discussion and answers, then reflect the figure to confirm the answer. Repeat this demonstration process using the right-left diagonal axis.

GUIDED PRACTICE:

EXERCISES: **B-70, B-73, B-77, B-80**

Give students sufficient time to complete these exercises. Then, using the demonstration methodology above, have them discuss and explain their choices. If students have difficulty visualizing the reflections, make transparency drawings of the figures to confirm the answers.

ANSWERS:

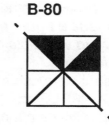

B-70   B-73   B-77   B-80

INDEPENDENT PRACTICE:

Assign exercises **B-71** and **B-72**, **B-74** through **B-76**, **B-78** and **B-79**, **B-81** through **B-83**

DISCUSSION TIPS:

The key word in this exercise is **reflection**. Ask students to identify examples of reflection, e.g., mirrors, water surfaces, and polished surfaces. If students have difficulty visualizing reflections, encourage them to sketch the figure, cut it out, and reflect it about the required axis. Some figures are provided on TM #24 for this purpose.

ANSWERS:

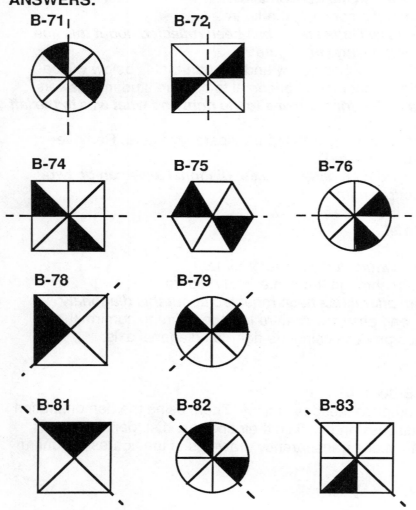

B-71   B-72

B-74   B-75   B-76

B-78   B-79

B-81   B-82   B-83

FOLLOW-UP REFERENT:
> *When might you need to predict how a shape or pattern will look when it has been reflected?*

Examples: putting together models or dress patterns; tasks which require mirror perception, e.g., applying makeup, shaving, tying neckties, styling, combing, or parting hair; using a rearview mirror in an automobile

CURRICULUM APPLICATION:
Language Arts: letter discrimination
Mathematics: similarity and congruence exercises; recognizing fractional parts; reflection
    as a common concept in geometry
Science: recognizing symmetry in nature, e.g., shell patterns, position and structure of
    leaves; model building; concepts of optics and momentum in physics
Social Studies: spatial orientation in map reading; recognizing or producing graphs that
    show positive and negative changes
Enrichment Areas: career education discussions involving architecture, engineering,
    construction, drafting, graphic design, dental practice, radiology, archaeology; design
    principles in drawing, relief sculpture, printmaking, photography, and making molds;
    drafting and architectural drawing; reading blueprints

EXTENDING ACTIVITIES:
None.

MULTIPLE REFLECTIONS—SUPPLY

STRAND: Figural Sequences   **PAGES:** 122–127

ADDITIONAL MATERIALS:
Transparencies of TMs #24 and #25

INTRODUCTION:
> *In the previous exercise you shaded a figure to show how it looked after a single-axis reflection.*

OBJECTIVE:
> *In these exercises you will show how a figure looks when it has been reflected about several axes.*

DEMONSTRATION/EXPLANATION:
Project figure **A** from TM #25, then reflect it about the vertical axis.
> *This is how the pattern looks when it has been reflected once about the vertical axis.*

Return the pattern to its original position.
> *Figures may be reflected more than once. How would this figure look if it were reflected three times about the vertical axis?*

Allow students time to visualize the multiple reflection and discuss their answers, then demonstrate the move, having students count each time you reflect the figure. Replace figure **A** with figure **B** and reflect it once about the horizontal axis.

> *This is how this pattern looks when it has been reflected once about the horizontal axis.*

Reflect the pattern again horizontally.

> *This is a double horizontal reflection...*

Repeat the reflection.

> *...and this is a triple. Notice how the pattern repeats.*

Return the figure to its original position.

> *What if you wanted to do several different reflections? How would this figure look if it were reflected once about the vertical, then once about the horizontal?*

Allow time for discussion and answers, then demonstrate the reflections in the order mentioned to confirm student answers. Replace figure **B** with figure **C**.

> *A third axis for reflection is the top-left to bottom-right diagonal axis.*

Place a pencil over figure **C** to show the axis location, then reflect figure **C** once about the diagonal axis and return it to its original position.

> *Notice how the pattern changes for double and triple diagonal reflections.*

Repeat the reflection slowly so students can observe changes. Encourage students to verbalize their observations, then illustrate multiple reflections about the top-right to lower-left diagonal. Again, encourage observations.

> *How would this figure look if you reflected it once about each diagonal—first the top left-bottom right, then the top right-bottom left?*

Allow time for discussion and projections. Encourage students to sketch the progression on scrap paper, then demonstrate the described reflection.

> *In each of the following exercises, you will be asked to show patterns resulting from multiple reflections. Some of these will combine reflections about different axes, so pay close attention to the location and direction of the dotted axis lines.*

GUIDED PRACTICE:
EXERCISES: **B-84, B-85**
Give students sufficient time to complete these exercises, then have them discuss and explain their choices. Figure **E** may be cut from TM #24 to confirm student answers.
ANSWERS:

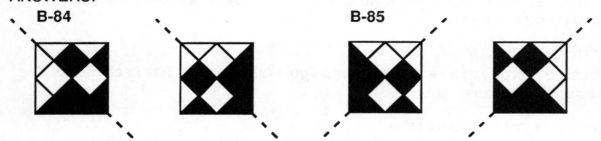

INDEPENDENT PRACTICE:
Assign exercises **B-86** through **B-95**

DISCUSSION TIPS:
The key word in this exercise is **reflection**. Ask students to identify examples of reflection

in their surroundings, e.g., mirrors, water surfaces, and polished surfaces. Some figures in these exercises are reproduced on TM #24 and may be used to demonstrate and/or confirm student answers.

ANSWERS:

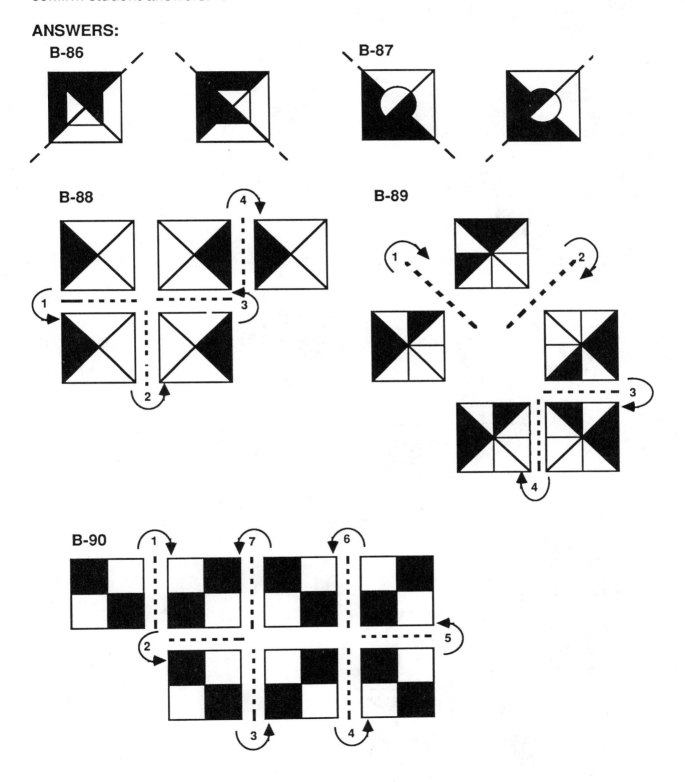

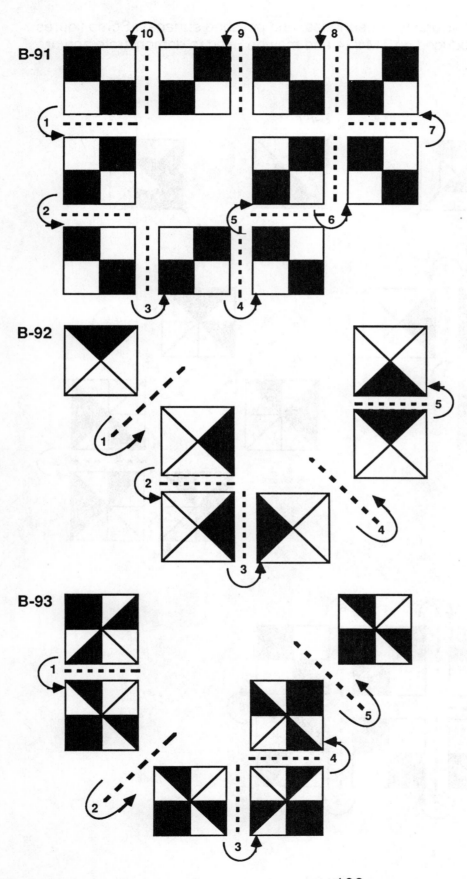

B-91

B-92

B-93

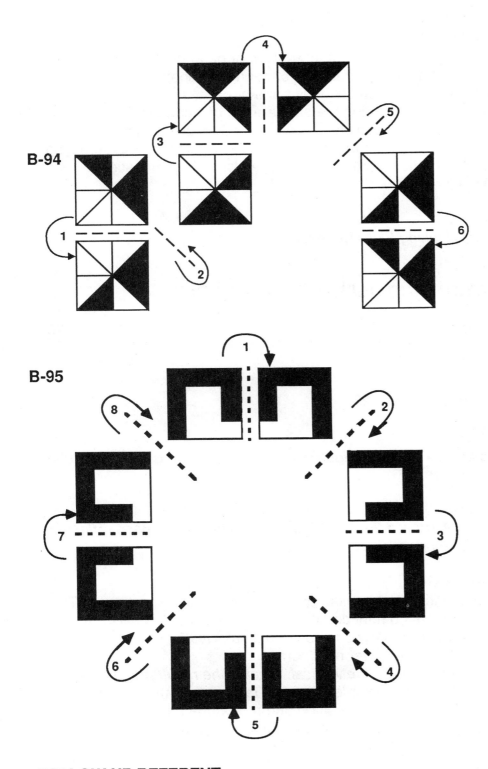

B-94

B-95

FOLLOW-UP REFERENT:
When might you need to predict how a shape or pattern will look after it has been reflected about one or more given axes?
Examples: assembling models or pattern pieces

CURRICULUM APPLICATION:
Language Arts: creating symmetrical designs for journalism or other creative projects
Mathematics: predicting results of multiple reflections of geometric shapes
Science: completing illustrations of symmetrical body parts or organs
Social Studies: drawing conclusions regarding the appearance of incomplete artifacts
Enrichment Areas: career education discussions involving architecture, engineering,
    construction, drafting, graphic design, dental practice, radiology, archaeology; creating
    drill team or marching band formations; creating floor exercises for gymnastics
    exhibitions; taking visual aptitude tests

EXTENDING ACTIVITIES:
Figure Relations B, *Inductive Thinking Skills* Series, pp. 18–21

ROTATION AND REFLECTION—SUPPLY

STRAND: Figural Sequences   **PAGES:** 128–129

ADDITIONAL MATERIALS:
Transparency of TM #25 (figure **D**)
Transparency of student workbook page 128

INTRODUCTION:
In the previous exercise you shaded a figure to show how it would look after it had been reflected several times.

OBJECTIVE:
In these exercises you will draw a figure as it will look when it has been reflected, then rotated—or rotated, then reflected.

DEMONSTRATION/EXPLANATION:
Project figure **D** (**EXAMPLE**, student workbook page 128) from the transparency of TM #25, placing the black section in the top right corner.
How will this figure look if you rotate it one position clockwise?
Answer: The black section will be in the lower right corner.
Now reflect this rotated figure about the vertical. What is the resulting pattern?
Answer: The black square will be in the lower left corner. Demonstrate the movement to confirm answer. Return pattern to its original position and repeat the above steps using different rotation/reflection combinations until students can do the process mentally.

GUIDED PRACTICE:
EXERCISES: **B-96, B-97**
Give students sufficient time to complete these exercises. Then, using the demonstration methodology above, have them discuss and explain their choices.

ANSWERS:
B-96

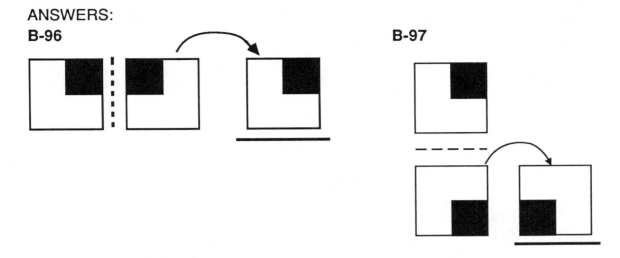

B-97

INDEPENDENT PRACTICE:
Assign exercises **B-98** through **B-102**

DISCUSSION TIPS:
Stress that the operations are to be done *in the order stated*. If students have difficulty arriving at the correct answer, have them describe or sketch the changes for each step.

ANSWERS:

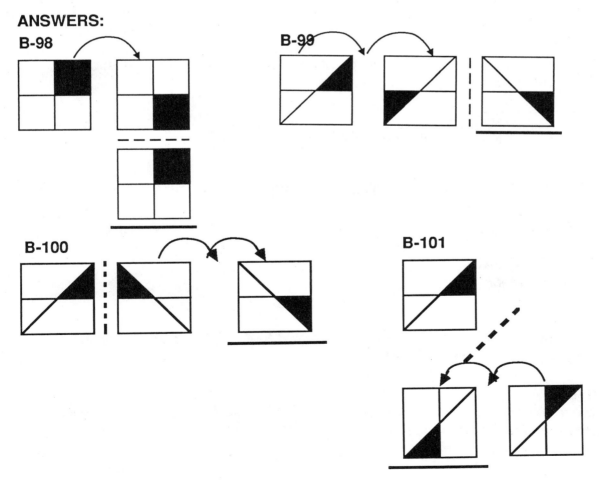

B-98

B-99

B-100

B-101

B-102

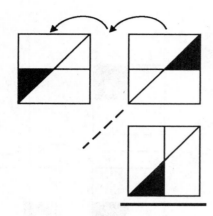

FOLLOW-UP REFERENT:

When might you need to predict how a shape or pattern will look when it has been both rotated and reflected?

Examples: assembling models, dress patterns, or jigsaw puzzles

CURRICULUM APPLICATION:

Language Arts: creating symmetrical designs for journalism or other creative projects
Mathematics: predicting results of multiple reflections of geometric shapes
Science: completing illustrations of symmetrical body parts or organs
Social Studies: drawing conclusions regarding the appearance of incomplete artifacts
Enrichment Areas: career education discussions involving architecture, engineering, construction, drafting, graphic design, dental practice, radiology, archaeology; creating drill team or marching band formations; creating floor exercises for gymnastics exhibitions; visual apptitude tests

EXTENDING ACTIVITIES:

Figure Relations B, *Inductive Thinking Skills* Series, pp. 14–17

EXPLAINING ROTATION OR REFLECTION

STRAND: Figural Sequences   **PAGES:** 130–131

ADDITIONAL MATERIALS:

Transparency of TM #26

INTRODUCTION:

In the previous exercise you drew a figure as it looked after it was reflected, then rotated—or rotated, then reflected.

OBJECTIVE:

In these exercises you are given two figures and asked to explain what has been done to the first figure to change it into the second figure.

DEMONSTRATION/EXPLANATION:
Project figures **A** and **B** from TM #26.

> *Here are two views of the same figure. What would you do to figure **A** to make it look like figure **B**?*

Allow time for discussion. Have students demonstrate their answers by moving the cutout pattern from the transparency in the manner suggested. Answer: The figure has been rotated one position counterclockwise (to the left). Change the cover sheet to project only figures **A** and **C**.

> *Here are two other views of the same figure. What would you do to figure **A** to make it look like figure **C**?*

Allow time for discussion. Have students demonstrate their answers by moving the cutout pattern. Answer: The figure has been reflected about the horizontal axis. Change the cover sheet to project only figures **C** and **D**.

> *Here are two other views of the same figure. What would you do to figure **C** to make it look like figure **D**?*

Allow time for discussion. Have students demonstrate their answers by moving the cutout pattern. Answer: The figure has been reflected about a diagonal (top left to bottom right) axis. Change the cover sheet to project only figures **B** and **D**.

> *Here are two other views of the same figure. What would you do to figure **B** to make it look like figure **D**?*

Allow time for discussion. Have students demonstrate their answers by moving the cutout pattern. Answer: The figure has been rotated two positions clockwise (to the right).

GUIDED PRACTICE:
EXERCISES: **B-103, B-104**
Give students sufficient time to complete these exercises, then have them discuss and explain their choices.
ANSWERS:
B-103 Rotated: <u>no</u>; Reflected: <u>yes</u>; Axis: <u>vertical</u>
B-104 Rotated: <u>yes</u>; Number of positions: <u>one</u>; Direction: <u>right</u>; Reflected: <u>no</u>

INDEPENDENT PRACTICE:
Assign exercises **B-105** through **B-112**

DISCUSSION TIPS:
Alternate answers are possible, especially for rotations. Have students explain their answers as follows: "The first figure has been _____ to produce the second figure." For example: "The first figure has been <u>reflected about a left-right diagonal axis</u> to produce the second figure." or "The first figure has been <u>rotated two positions to the left</u> to produce the second figure."

ANSWERS:
B-105 Rotated: <u>yes</u>; Direction: <u>left</u>; Number of positions: <u>one</u>; Reflected: <u>no</u>
B-106 Rotated: <u>yes</u>; Number of positions: <u>two</u>; Direction: <u>left or right</u>; Reflected: <u>no</u>
B-107 Rotated: <u>no</u>; Reflected: <u>yes</u>; Axis: <u>horizontal</u>
B-108 Rotated: <u>yes</u>; Number of positions: <u>one</u>; Direction: <u>right</u>; Reflected: <u>no</u>
B-109 Rotated: <u>no</u>; Reflected: <u>yes</u>; Axis: <u>diagonal</u>

B-110 Rotated: <u>no</u>; Reflected: <u>yes</u>; Axis: <u>vertical</u>
B-111 Rotated: <u>no</u>; Reflected: <u>yes</u>; Axis: <u>horizontal</u>
B-112 Rotated: <u>no</u>; Reflected: <u>yes</u>; Axis: <u>diagonal</u>

FOLLOW-UP REFERENT:
> *When might you need to explain how a shape or pattern has been rotated or reflected?*

Examples: assembling (or giving instructions for assembling) models or dress patterns; tasks requiring mirror perception, e.g., applying makeup, tying neckties; using a rearview mirror in an automobile

CURRICULUM APPLICATION:
Language Arts: letter discrimination
Mathematics: similarity and congruence exercises; recognizing fractional parts; reflection and rotation as common concepts in geometry
Science: observing reflected patterns in the spirals of shells, the position and structure of leaves, and other examples of symmetry in nature; model building; optics and momentum concepts in physics; rotation of the earth; analysis of forces causing rotation
Social Studies: changing the orientation of maps
Enrichment Areas: career education discussions involving architecture, engineering, construction, drafting, graphic design, dental practice, radiology, archaeology; design principles in drawing, relief sculpture, printmaking, photography, and making molds; drafting and architectural drawing; reading blueprints; visual apptitude tests

EXTENDING ACTIVITIES:
<u>Figure Relations B</u>, *Inductive Thinking Skills* Series, pp. 22–28

PAPER FOLDING—SELECT

STRAND: Figural Sequences   **PAGES:** 132–139

ADDITIONAL MATERIALS:
Transparency of TM #27
Student handouts of TM #27
Scissors

INTRODUCTION:
NOTE: In paper-folding exercises the word **pattern** *refers to the folded item; the word* **design** *refers to the unfolded item.*
> *Have you ever noticed that when you cut a design in a folded paper pattern it looks different after it has been unfolded than it did when you cut the pattern?*

As students observe, cut a fancy, sharply curved pattern from folded scrap paper. Project the pattern, then unfold the paper on the overhead projector.
> *When you unfold the pattern, you have a lovely design. Now two sides have the same curves as the one edge that was cut.*

Fold the paper again. Select a noticeable curve and point as you explain.
> *This curve...*

Slowly open the pattern.
> *...becomes two curves.*

OBJECTIVE:
> *In these exercises you will identify the pattern which produced a particular design.*

DEMONSTRATION/EXPLANATION:
Project TM #27. Distribute copies of TM #27 and have students cut out figures **1**, **2**, and **3**. Punch out the holes with a hole punch or a pencil. Point to design **1**.
> *Which pattern—a, b, or c—will unfold to make design 1?*

Answer: **c**
> *Why can't pattern a be the answer? Look carefully at the dotted line which represents the fold line.*

Answer: The fold line is on the wrong side.
> *Why can't pattern b be the answer?*

Answer: In pattern **b** the three holes are aligned diagonally.
> *How can you be certain that c is the right choice?*

Answer: Fold design **1** and match it to pattern **c**.
> *Which pattern—a, b, or c—will make design 2 when it is unfolded?*

Answer: **a**
> *Why can't patterns b or c be the answer?*

Answer: In pattern **b** the three holes are aligned diagonally. Pattern **c** has the fold line on the wrong side.
> *How can you be sure that a is the right choice?*

Answer: Fold design **2** and match it to pattern **a**.
> *Which pattern—a, b, or c—will make design 3 when it is unfolded?*

Answer: **b**
> *How can you be sure that b is the right choice?*

Answer: Fold design **3** and match it to pattern **b**.
> *The design in exercise B-113 on page 132 is similar to one you have just finished.*
> *Which pattern on the right will unfold to make this design?*

Answer: **c**

GUIDED PRACTICE:
EXERCISES: **B-114, B-115, B-116, B-117**
Give students sufficient time to complete these exercises. Then, using the demonstration methodology above, have them discuss and explain their choices. Have students make models of any patterns they find difficult. *NOTE: In exercises **B-114** through **B-132** students select the pattern which will unfold to create a given design. In exercises **B-133** through **B-152** students reverse this process, selecting the design which results from unfolding a given pattern.*
ANSWERS: **B-114** e; **B-115** a; **B-116** b; **B-117** d

INDEPENDENT PRACTICE:
Assign exercises **B-118** through **B-152**

DISCUSSION TIPS:
It is necessary that students distinguish folded edges from outer edges. Identify these distinctions and encourage students to use the directional words **right**, **left**, and **center**. **Inner**, **outer**, and **near** are relative terms requiring some point for comparison. You may want to include the concepts of **curve** and **symmetry**.

ANSWERS:
B-118 a; **B-119** e; **B-120** d; **B-121** b; **B-122** c
B-123 c; **B-124** d; **B-125** a; **B-126** e; **B-127** b
B-128 d; **B-129** e; **B-130** a; **B-131** b; **B-132** c
B-133 d; **B-134** a; **B-135** e; **B-136** b; **B-137** c
B-138 c; **B-139** d; **B-140** a; **B-141** e; **B-142** b
B-143 b; **B-144** d; **B-145** e; **B-146** a; **B-147** c
B-148 d; **B-149** e; **B-150** a; **B-151** b; **B-152** c

FOLLOW-UP REFERENT:
> *When might you need to match patterns and designs?*

Examples: refolding a map; cutting or copying paper snowflake designs; finding corresponding pattern pieces in sewing, wood, or metal working

CURRICULUM APPLICATION:
Language Arts: doing word search puzzles; recognizing sound or letter patterns
Mathematics: visual perception skills; symmetry exercises; forming geometric patterns
Science: determining symmetry in natural forms; producing symmetrically shaped
  diagrams, e.g., flowers, insects, organs; predicting appearance or position of stars or
  planets; reproducing crystal or snowflake patterns
Social Studies: seeing patterns in charts, graphs, or schedules
Enrichment Areas: art projects involving symmetry; creating computer-generated
  designs; breaking down dance routines or art projects into groups of steps

EXTENDING ACTIVITIES:
Paper patterns with two lines of symmetry

PAPER FOLDING—SUPPLY

STRAND: Figural Sequences   **PAGES:** 140–145

ADDITIONAL MATERIALS:
Paper model of exercise **B-153**, student workbook page 140

INTRODUCTION:
> *In the previous exercise you matched given patterns with designs.*

OBJECTIVE:
> *In these exercises you will draw either the pattern that makes a given design or the design that results from unfolding a given pattern.*

DEMONSTRATION/EXPLANATION:

Hold up the paper model of exercise **B-153**.

This model is the design from exercise B-153 on page 140.

Draw a vertical rectangle on the chalkboard, making the left side a dotted line.

When the fold line is on the left, the pattern will open like a book. You must decide where the holes should be placed in the pattern to make this design.

Pause for student opinions and discussion. Draw in holes as students suggest, allowing discussion of each possible answer. Answer: One hole near the top outside corner, one hole near the top inside corner, and one hole near the bottom inside corner.

GUIDED PRACTICE:

EXERCISES: **B-154, B-155**

Give students sufficient time to complete these exercises. Then, using the demonstration methodology above, have them discuss and explain their choices. Make models of any designs that present problems. *NOTE: In exercises* **B-154** *through* **B-166**, *students will draw the pattern produced by folding a design. In exercises* **B-167** *through* **B-180** *they will reverse the process, drawing the design which results from unfolding a pattern.*

ANSWERS:

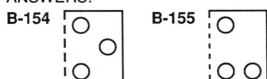

INDEPENDENT PRACTICE:

Assign exercises **B-156** through **B-180**

DISCUSSION TIPS:

Encourage students to distinguish folded edges from outer edges and to use directional words: **right**, **left**, and **center**. **Inner**, **outer**, and **near** are relative terms requiring some point for comparison. Emphasize and encourage use of **contrasts**: right/left/center, inner/outer, top/bottom, edge/fold, pattern/design (folded/unfolded), symmetry (optional).

ANSWERS:

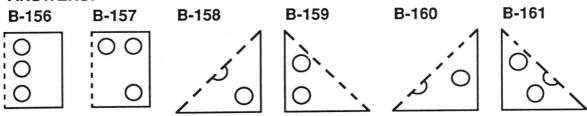

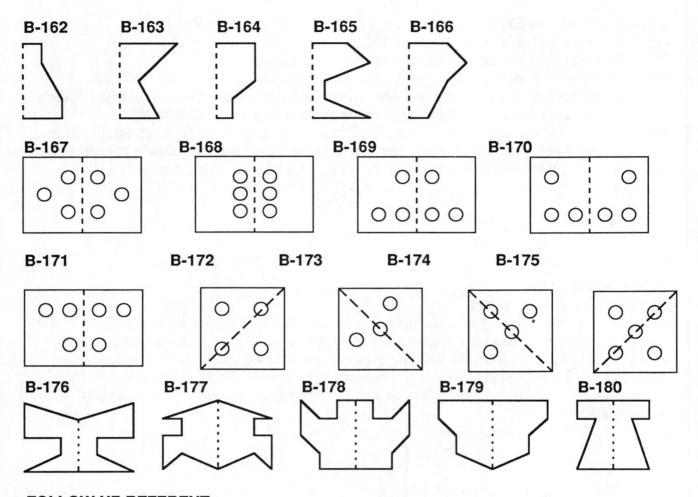

FOLLOW-UP REFERENT:
When might you need to visualize or draw how something will look after it has been folded or unfolded?

Examples: folding linens or clothing to fit a shelf or drawer; paper cutting; symmetry in cut patterns; finding and combining pattern pieces

CURRICULUM APPLICATION:
Language Arts: doing word search puzzles; recognizing sound or letter patterns
Mathematics: visual perception skills; symmetry exercises; forming geometric patterns
Science: producing crystal or snowflake patterns on paper; producing symmetrically
  shaped diagrams, e.g., flowers, insects, organs; determining symmetry in natural forms;
  predicting appearance or position of stars or planets
Social Studies: map drawing skills; seeing patterns in charts, graphs, or schedules
Enrichment Areas: art projects involving symmetry; creating computer-generated
  designs; breaking down dance routines or art projects into groups of steps; memorizing
  printed music patterns

EXTENDING ACTIVITIES:
None.

TWO-AXIS PAPER FOLDING—SELECT

STRAND: Figural Sequences   **PAGES:** 146–156

ADDITIONAL MATERIALS:
Paper model of the **EXAMPLE**, student workbook page 146

INTRODUCTION:
NOTE: **Pattern** *refers to the folded item;* **design** *refers to the unfolded item.*
In previous exercises you selected and drew designs or patterns that resulted from folding or unfolding along a single axis. That is, the pattern was unfolded only once to produce a design.

OBJECTIVE:
In these exercises the patterns have been folded twice. You will select the pattern that results when a design is folded twice or the design that results when a pattern is unfolded twice.

DEMONSTRATION/EXPLANATION:
Hold up the paper model of the **EXAMPLE** from page 146.
If you fold this design first along the vertical axis...
Hold up the single-folded pattern with the fold to the left.
...then along the horizontal axis,...
Hold up the twice-folded pattern with the folds to the left and the bottom.
...your will get a pattern like pattern b. What would happen if you folded the design in the reverse order—along the horizontal axis first, then along the vertical axis?
Discussion. Have students verify their answers by folding the design.

GUIDED PRACTICE:
EXERCISES: **B-181, B-182, B-183**
Give students sufficient time to complete these exercises, then have them discuss, explain, and, if necessary, demonstrate their answers. *NOTE: In exercises* **B-181** *through* **B-195**, *students will select the pattern produced by folding a design. In exercises* **B-196** *through* **B-216**, *they will reverse the process, selecting the design which results from unfolding a pattern.*
ANSWERS: **B-181** d; **B-182** b; **B-183** c

INDEPENDENT PRACTICE:
Assign exercises **B-184** through **B-216**
NOTE: You may wish to assign exercises **B-184** *through* **B-195** *(folding) one day and* **B-196** *through* **B-216** *(unfolding) the next day.*

DISCUSSION TIPS:
Students must distinguish folded edges from outer edges. Identify these and encourage students to use the directional words **right**, **left**, and **center**. **Inner**, **outer**, and **near** are relative terms that require some point for comparison. Emphasize and repeat these **contrasts**: right/left/center, inner/outer, top/bottom, pattern/design (folded/unfolded), edge/fold, symmetry (optional).

ANSWERS:
B-184 c; B-185 b; B-186 b; B-187 d; B-188 c; B-189 e; B-190 a; B-191 b; B-192 d;
B-193 c; B-194 a; B-195 b
B-196 b; B-197 c; B-198 a; B-199 b; B-200 b; B-201 c; B-202 a
B-203 c; B-204 a; B-205 b; B-206 d; B-207 b; B-208 c; B-209 a; B-210 d;
B-211 b; B-212 a; B-213 c; B-214 a; B-215 b; B-216 c

FOLLOW-UP REFERENT:
When might you need to visualize how something will look after it has been folded or unfolded along two axes?
Examples: folding linens or clothing to fit a shelf or drawer; paper cutting; symmetry in cut patterns; finding and combining pattern pieces

CURRICULUM APPLICATION:
Language Arts: doing word search puzzles; recognizing sound or letter patterns
Mathematics: visual perception skills; symmetry exercises; forming geometric patterns
Science: determining symmetry in natural forms; producing symmetrically shaped
   diagrams, e.g., flowers, insects, organs; reproducing crystal or snowflake patterns on
   paper; predicting appearance or position of stars or planets
Social Studies: seeing patterns in charts, graphs, or schedules
Enrichment Areas: art projects involving symmetry; creating computer-generated
   designs; memorizing printed music patterns; breaking down dance routines or art
   projects into groups of steps

EXTENDING ACTIVITIES:
None.

TWO-AXIS PAPER FOLDING—SUPPLY

STRAND: Figural Sequences   **PAGES:** 157–163

ADDITIONAL MATERIALS:
Paper model of the **EXAMPLE**, student workbook page 157

INTRODUCTION:
NOTE: **Pattern** *refers to the folded item;* **design** *to the unfolded item.*
   In the previous exercise you selected designs or patterns that resulted from folding
   or unfolding along two axes.

OBJECTIVE:
   In these exercises the designs are also to be folded twice. You will draw the
   pattern that results from folding a design twice, or you will draw the design that
   results from unfolding a pattern twice.

DEMONSTRATION/EXPLANATION:
Hold up the paper model of the **EXAMPLE** from page 157. The fold lines should be
drawn on the design.

If you fold this design first along the vertical axis...
Hold up the single-folded pattern with the fold to the left.
...then along the horizontal axis...
Hold up the twice-folded pattern with the folds on the left and the bottom.
...and hold the pattern this way, it looks like view a in the EXAMPLE on page 157. Notice which edges are folded and which are cut. The fold lines are to the left and the bottom of the pattern. View b is the reflected pattern. Where are the fold lines?
Answer: To the right and the bottom. Turn your model pattern to match view **b** and show it to the students, indicating the fold lines.
View c calls for the fold lines to be in a different position again. This time they are to the top and left.
Turn the model to illustrate the change, then reflect it about the vertical to match view **d**.
Where are the fold lines in this view?
Answer: To the top and right.
The location of the fold lines is important in determining how a pattern looks.

GUIDED PRACTICE:
EXERCISES: **B-217, B-218**
Give students sufficient time to complete these exercises, then have them explain and model their responses. *NOTE: In exercises B-217 through B-229, students will draw the patterns produced by folding a design twice. In exercises B-230 through B-241 students will reverse the process, drawing the design which results when a twice-folded pattern is unfolded.*
ANSWERS:

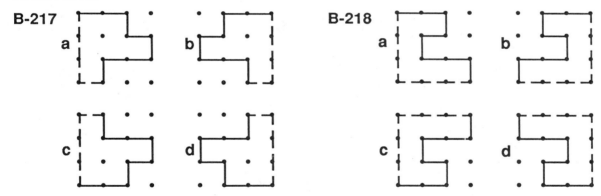

INDEPENDENT PRACTICE:
Assign exercises **B-219** through **B-241**
NOTE: You may wish to assign exercises B-219 through B-229 (folding) one day and B-230 through B-241 (unfolding) the next day.

DISCUSSION TIPS:
Students must distinguish folded edges from outer edges. Identify these distinctions and encourage students to use directional and relative terms: **right, left, center, inner, outer,** and **near.** Students should describe their drawing accurately, using the dot locations and number of spaces as reference points.

ANSWERS:

NOTE: Exercises B-222 through B-229 have four possible correct answers.

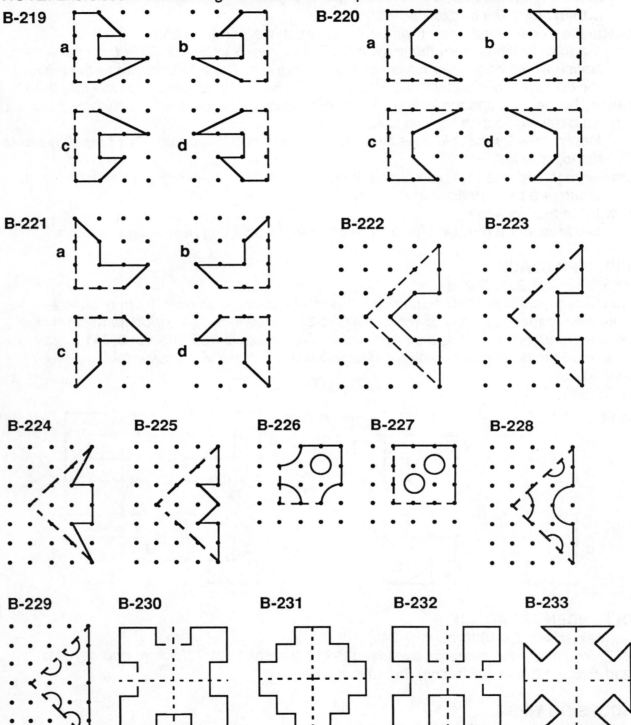

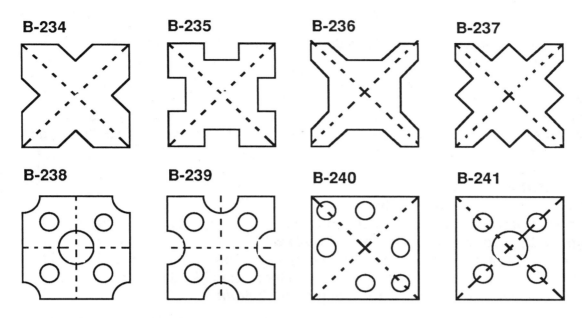

FOLLOW-UP REFERENT:

When might you need to recognize how something will look after it has been folded or unfolded along two axes?

Examples: folding linens or clothing to fit a shelf or drawer; paper cutting; symmetry in cut patterns; finding and combining pattern pieces

CURRICULUM APPLICATION:

Language Arts: doing word search puzzles; recognizing sound or letter patterns

Mathematics: visual perception skills; symmetry exercises; forming geometric patterns

Science: determining symmetry in natural forms; producing symmetrically shaped
   diagrams, e.g., flowers, insects, organs; reproducing crystal or snowflake patterns on
   paper; predicting appearance or position of stars or planets

Social Studies: seeing patterns in charts, graphs, or schedules

Enrichment Areas: art projects involving symmetry; creating computer-generated
   designs; memorizing printed music patterns; breaking down dance routines or art
   projects into groups of steps

EXTENDING ACTIVITIES:

None.

PATTERN FOLDING—SELECT/MATCHING

STRAND: Figural Sequences   **PAGES:** 164–170

ADDITIONAL MATERIALS:

Shoe box

Paper wrapper pattern for the shoe box

Transparency of student workbook page 164

INTRODUCTION:
In previous exercises you mentally folded and unfolded paper and drew the resulting pattern or design.

OBJECTIVE:
In these exercises you will also mentally fold paper, but this time the folded paper will become a box or a solid. You will identify which solid or box can be wrapped by or made from a given pattern.

DEMONSTRATION/EXPLANATION:
Hold up the wrapper pattern and the box.
Here is a box and a paper pattern. Do you think this pattern can be wrapped around the box, covering the whole surface exactly?
Allow time for discussion and predictions, then wrap the pattern around the box. Unfold the wrapper, mark the fold lines so students can see them, and identify pairs of parts.
Notice that two pieces like this cover the top and bottom,...
Point.
...two like this cover the ends,...
Point.
...and two like this cover the sides.
Project the **EXAMPLE** exercise from the transparency of student workbook page 164.
This pattern is somewhat like our box. It also has three pairs of matching sides.
Indicate the matching parts, then hold up the wrapper pattern used for the shoe box.
How does this pattern differ from the shoe-box pattern?
Answer: It is a pattern for a shorter box, more like a shirt box.
*All the solids shown are box-like. Is **a** the correct solid for the wrapper?*
Answer: No; solid **a** is deep enough and wide enough, but not long enough.
*Does solid **b** match the wrapper?*
Answer: No; it is too tall.
*Solid **c** has the correct proportions for the wrapper to fit and has been circled.*

GUIDED PRACTICE:
EXERCISE: **B-242**
Give students sufficient time to complete this exercise. Then, using the demonstration methodology above, have them discuss and explain their choice.
ANSWER: **B-242** b

INDEPENDENT PRACTICE:
Assign exercises **B-243** through **B-259**

DISCUSSION TIPS:
If students have difficulty visualizing how a pattern will look when folded, have them create patterns or disassemble cardboard boxes. Encourage students to explain why the alternate answers do not fit the pattern.

ANSWERS:
B-243 a; B-244 c; B-245 b; B-246 a; B-247 b; B-248 c

B-249 d; **B-250** b; **B-251** a; **B-252** c; **B-253** a; **B-254** d; **B-255** b;
B-256 b; **B-257** d; **B-258** a; **B-259** c

FOLLOW-UP REFERENT:
When might you need to recognize which solid can be wrapped or created by a given pattern?
Examples: model building; wrapping gifts or packages; upholstering furniture; cardboard carpentry

CURRICULUM APPLICATION:
Language Arts: ————————
Mathematics: visual perception skills; surface area problems
Science: reproducing models of crystals
Social Studies: modeling globes or other three-dimensional map projects
Enrichment Areas: art and industrial arts projects involving covering surfaces

EXTENDING ACTIVITIES:
None.

SELECTING/MATCHING PATTERN PIECES

STRAND: Figural Sequences   **PAGES:** 171–175

ADDITIONAL MATERIALS:
Transparency of student workbook page 172
Washable transparency marker
Rectangular box
Paper pattern pieces—some that fit the faces of the box and some that do not

INTRODUCTION:
In the previous exercise you selected or matched wrapper patterns to solids.

OBJECTIVE:
In these exercises you will choose those pattern pieces which will cover all the faces of a solid or box.

DEMONSTRATION/EXPLANATION:
Hold up one piece of the paper wrapper pattern and the box.
Look at this box and piece of paper. Will this paper fit on one face of the box?
Allow time for discussion and prediction. Encourage students to explain why the piece will or will not fit and to specify which surface they think it will cover. Continue in the same manner with other pattern pieces until all have been tested.
How many different shapes are needed to complete a wrapper pattern for this rectangular box?
Answer: Three different sized rectangles.
How many of each size are needed?

Answer: Two of each size are needed, or three pairs. Project the **EXAMPLE** from the transparency of student workbook page 172.

How is the box shown in this EXAMPLE different from the box we just covered?

Answer: The ends of the **EXAMPLE** box are square. (Other variations may also exist.)

How many squares do you need to cover or make the ends?

Answer: Two. Circle the **2** inside the square pattern on the right.

What do you notice about the front and the top of this box?

Answer: They are the same size.

If the front and top are the same size and the box is rectangular, what do you know about the sides you can't see—the back and the bottom?

Answer: They are the same size as the sides opposite them.

How many rectangles do you need to finish the box?

Answer: Four. Circle the **4** inside the rectangle.

Why have the other pieces been crossed out?

Answer: They are all too big.

GUIDED PRACTICE:

EXERCISES: **B-260, B-261, B-262**

Give students sufficient time to complete these exercises. Then, using the demonstration methodology above, have them discuss and explain their choices. Encourage them to explain why the crossed-out pieces were eliminated.

ANSWERS:

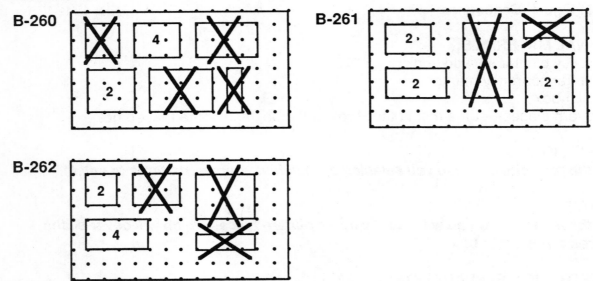

INDEPENDENT PRACTICE:

Assign exercises **B-263** through **B-274**

DISCUSSION TIPS:

If students have difficulty visualizing pattern pieces, have them disassemble cardboard boxes or duplicate and fold patterns using scrap paper.

ANSWERS:

B-263

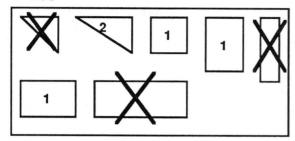

B-264

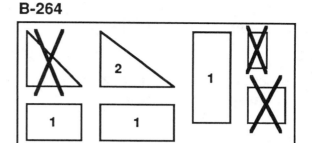

B-265

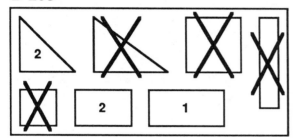

B-266

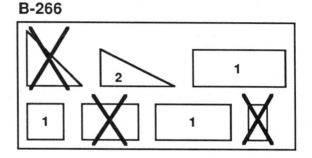

B-267 Use <u>2</u> of side **a** and <u>4</u> of side **d**

B-268 Use <u>4</u> of side **e** and <u>2</u> of side **f**

B-269 Use <u>2</u> of side **b**, <u>2</u> of side **d**, and <u>2</u> of side **e**

B-270 Use <u>2</u> of side **b**, <u>2</u> of side **g**, and <u>2</u> of side **h**

B-271 Use <u>1</u> each of sides **b**, **c**, **f**, and **g** and <u>2</u> of side **j**

B-272 Use <u>1</u> each of sides **a**, **c**, **d**, and **e** and <u>2</u> of side **h**

B-273 Use <u>1</u> each of sides **b**, **c**, **e**, and **f** and <u>2</u> of side **i**

B-274 Use <u>1</u> each of side **e** and **g** and <u>2</u> each of sides **c** and **k**

FOLLOW-UP REFERENT:

When might you need to recognize the pattern pieces that will make a given item?
Examples: model building; construction toys; clothing or woodworking construction

CURRICULUM APPLICATION:

Language Arts: ―――――――
Mathematics: visual perception skills; surface area problems
Science: producing models of crystals or other patterned three-dementional objects
Social Studies: modeling globes or other three-dimensional map projects
Enrichment Areas: art and industrial arts projects involving covering surfaces or making
  a pattern

EXTENDING ACTIVITIES:

None.

PRODUCE A PATTERN

STRAND: Figural Sequences   **PAGES:** 176–178

ADDITIONAL MATERIALS:
Transparency of student workbook page 176
Washable transparency marker
Box
Paper for wrapping box

INTRODUCTION:
>*In the previous exercise you identified pattern pieces which matched the faces of different solids.*

OBJECTIVE:
>*In these exercises you will draw the wrapper pattern which will cover a given solid.*

DEMONSTRATION/EXPLANATION:
Hold up the box and paper.
>*Can you use this piece of paper to produce a wrapper pattern that will fit the sides of this box exactly?*

Answer: Place the box on the paper and trace around one side of the box. Demonstrate.
>*How can you continue the pattern?*

Answer: Tumble the box along the paper so each pattern piece touches the next one. If students do not mention the end pieces, direct their attention by holding up the drawn pattern and asking if it will wrap the box *entirely*. Make sure students understand that end pieces must be on opposite sides of the pattern. Continue until a wrapper pattern is produced.
>*How can you test this pattern?*

Answer: Cut it out and see if it covers the box. Project the transparency of page 176.
>*The box in exercise B-275 is somewhat like the box you just worked with. What is different about this solid?*

Pause for student answers.
>*The rectangle drawn on the grid to the right represents the pattern for the top of the box. How can the sides be drawn?*

Answer: Draw rectangles adjoining each of the four sides, each one space wide.
>*Where should the last pattern piece be drawn?*

Answer: Adjoining one of the rectangles that represents either the front or the back side of the box. It will be the same size as the given rectangle and located either at the top or the bottom of the wrapper pattern.

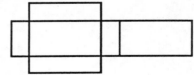

GUIDED PRACTICE:
EXERCISE: **B-276**

Give students sufficient time to complete this exercise. Then, using the demonstration methodology above, have them discuss and explain their drawing. *NOTE: Answer patterns will vary among students.*

ANSWER:

B-276

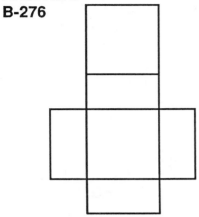

INDEPENDENT PRACTICE:
Assign exercises **B-277** through **B-282**

DISCUSSION TIPS:
If students have difficulty producing patterns, have them disassemble cardboard boxes or use scrap paper to reproduce and fold the patterns. Have students trace, cut, and fold any exercise answers which are unusual or doubtful.

ANSWERS:

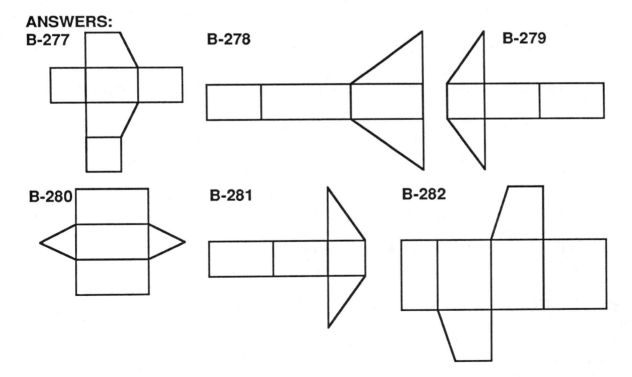

B-277   B-278   B-279

B-280   B-281   B-282

FOLLOW-UP REFERENT:
   When might you need to produce patterns for a given solid?
Examples: building models; manufacturing containers; upholstering furniture

CURRICULUM APPLICATION:
Language Arts: ——————
Mathematics: visual perception skills; surface area problems
Science: producing models of crystals or other patterned three-dimensional objects
Social Studies: modeling globes or other three-dimensional map projects
Enrichment Areas: art and industrial arts projects involving producing patterns and
    covering surfaces

EXTENDING ACTIVITIES:
None.

FOLDING CUBE PATTERNS—SELECT

STRAND: Figural Sequences   **PAGES:** 179–180

ADDITIONAL MATERIALS:
Paper patterns of the **EXAMPLE**, **B-283**, and **B-284**, student workbook page 179

INTRODUCTION:
> *In the previous exercise you selected pattern pieces that would produce a wrapper for a given solid or box.*

OBJECTIVE:
> *In these exercises you will identify patterns which can be folded into a cube.*

DEMONSTRATION/EXPLANATION:
Show students the cutout **EXAMPLE** pattern.
> *This pattern is like the EXAMPLE on page 179. Can someone fold it to produce a cube?*

Have a student volunteer demonstrate that folding the pattern will produce a cube. Hold up the pattern of exercise **B-283**.
> *Can this pattern be folded to produce a cube?*

Allow student volunteers to try folding the pattern. Answer: No.
> *Why not?*

Answer: Both flaps are on the same side, causing them to overlap and leave one face open. Hold up the pattern of exercise **B-284**.
> *Do you think this pattern be folded to produce a cube?*

Answer: Yes. Have a student demonstrate by folding the pattern.

GUIDED PRACTICE:
EXERCISES: **B-285, B-286**
Give students sufficient time to complete this exercise. Then, using the demonstration methodology above, have them discuss and explain their choices. Students may reproduce any patterns which give them difficulty.
ANSWERS: **B-285** Y; **B-286** N

INDEPENDENT PRACTICE:
Assign exercises **B-287** through **B-299**

DISCUSSION TIPS:
Since the exercises on page 180 have two variables (pattern and marking), they are more difficult than those on page 179. Some students may use the technique of identifying opposite faces; e.g., face **1** is opposite face **6**; face **2** is opposite face **4**; and face **3** is opposite face **5**. Thus, these pairs can never be next to one another in the pattern. In exercises **B-293** and **B-298** the patterns will not form cubes; **B-295** has the markings in the wrong locations.

ANSWERS:
B-287 N; **B-288** Y; **B-289** Y; **B-290** N; **B-291** Y; **B-292** N; **B-293** N (wrong pattern); **B-294** Y; **B-295** N (numbers in wrong locations); **B-296** Y; **B-297** Y; **B-298** N (wrong pattern); **B-299** Y

FOLLOW-UP REFERENT:
When might you need to recognize a pattern which will make a cube?
Examples: model building; pattern making; dice games; construction; assembling boxes; taking visual perception tests

CURRICULUM APPLICATION:
Language Arts: ——————
Mathematics: visual perception problems
Science: producing models of cubic crystals
Social Studies: ——————
Enrichment Areas: art and industrial arts projects involving covering cubes; pattern folding sections on standardized tests

EXTENDING ACTIVITIES:
None.

FOLDING CUBE PATTERNS—SUPPLY

STRAND: Figural Sequences   **PAGES:** 181–182

ADDITIONAL MATERIALS:
Transparency of student workbook page 181
Model of the cube on student workbook page 181 with faces marked

INTRODUCTION:
In the previous exercise you identified patterns which could be folded to make a given cube.

OBJECTIVE:
In these exercises you will number the blank faces of a pattern so it will match the given cube.

DEMONSTRATION/EXPLANATION:

Project exercise **B-300** from the transparency of page 181.

> *You are to mark the pattern in exercise* **B-300** *so it can be folded to match the picture of the cube at the top of the page. Start at the blank face above the face marked with a 3. The face below face 3 is marked with a 1. Which face of the cube is marked with a 1?*

Answer: The front face.

> *Which face is marked with a 3?*

Answer: The top face.

> *As you move up the pattern from 1 to 3 you are moving on the cube from the front face to the top face. If you continued moving in the same direction, which face on the cube would you come to next?*

Answer: The back face. If students have difficulty seeing this, show them a model of the block and tumble it forward to show the order of the exposed sides.

> *The cube at the top shows the back is marked with a 6, so you would mark the top face in the pattern with a 6. Now look at the blank face to the left of the face marked with a 1. As you move along the pattern from face 2 to face 1, in what direction are you moving on the cube?*

Answer: To the left.

> *If you continue in the same direction, what face would be next?*

Answer: Face **4** on the left side of the cube. Rotate the model about the vertical axis to demonstrate.

> *Mark the pattern piece to the left of the 1 with a 4. The remaining unmarked face is below the face marked with a 2. When this part of the pattern is folded, what part of the cube will it produce?*

Answer: The bottom.

> *Mark this face 5 to correspond with the number given for the bottom face.*

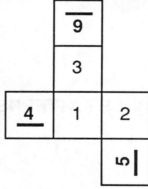

GUIDED PRACTICE:

EXERCISES: **B-301, B-302**

Give students sufficient time to complete these exercises. Then, using the demonstration methodology above, have them discuss and explain their choices.

ANSWERS:

B-301
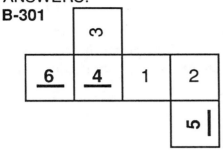

B-302
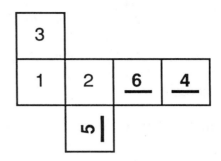

DISCUSSION TIPS:
Students should identify the missing faces and the direction they are moving as they proceed around the cube.

INDEPENDENT PRACTICE:
Assign exercises **B-303** through **B-307**

ANSWERS:
B-303   **B-304**   **B-305**

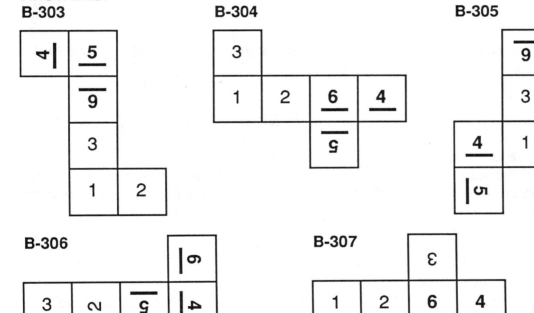

B-306   **B-307**

FOLLOW-UP REFERENT:
When might you need to recognize the relative position of the faces on a cube?
Examples: model building; assembling cardboard files, boxes, or display racks; games involving dice or construction

CURRICULUM APPLICATION:
Language Arts: organizing and presenting descriptions of solid shapes or figures
Mathematics: position discrimination involving cubes and prisms

Science: observing and recognizing different views of organisms or geological features

Social Studies: recognizing relative positions on three-dimensional maps

Enrichment Areas: career education discussions involving architecture, engineering, construction, drafting, graphic design, and archaeology; design principles for molds or sculptures; drafting and architectural drawing; reading blueprints; art and industrial arts projects

EXTENDING ACTIVITIES:
None.

ROTATING CUBES—SELECT/DESCRIBE/SUPPLY

STRAND: Figural Sequences   **PAGES:** 183–190

ADDITIONAL MATERIALS:
Transparency of student workbook page 185
Model of the cube on student workbook page 181 with faces marked

INTRODUCTION:
In the previous exercise you identified blank faces on a pattern so it could be folded to match a marked cube.

OBJECTIVE:
In these exercises you will predict which faces will appear as a cube is rotated.

DEMONSTRATION/EXPLANATION:
With your back to the students, hold up the cube model so they can see face **1**.
*Watch as this cube is rotated so the face marked **1** turns to where the faced marked **2** used to be.*
Rotate the cube in that manner.
What face is now visible?
Answer: The face marked **4**.
In which direction did the cube rotate?
Answer: To the right, because the **1** ends up on the right side of the cube. Return the cube to its original position.
This cube is marked like the one on page 181. Look at the relative positions of the numbers so you know where they all are before the cube is turned again. If the cube is rotated to the left, what number will be on the front face?
Answer: The **2**. *Do not turn the cube yet.*
Which number will then be on the left face?
Answer: The **1**. *Do not turn the cube yet.*
Which number will be on the right face?
Answer: The **6**. Demonstrate that the answer is correct. Return the cube to its original position.
Now the cube will be tumbled. If the cube is tumbled forward, what face will be on top?

Answer: The back, which is marked **6**. Demonstrate the move, then return the cube to its original position.

> *Again, starting with the 1, 2, and 3 showing, if the cube is tumbled backward, what face will be in front?*

Answer: The bottom, which is marked **5**. Demonstrate.

> *Again, starting with the 1, 2, and 3 showing, if the cube is tumbled to the left, what face will be on top?*

Answer: The right side, which is marked **2**. Demonstrate.

> *What number is now on the right side?*

Answer: **5**. Turn the cube so students can confirm the answer.

> *Again, starting with the 1, 2, and 3 showing, if the cube is tumbled to the right, what face will be on top?*

Answer: The left side, which is marked **4**. Project the transparency of page 185.

> *Look at the three cubes in the EXAMPLE. How can you tell that the cube has been rotated?*

Answer: The top numeral is the same, but points in a different direction. The front numeral changes.

> *How can you tell that a cube has been tumbled forward or backward?*

Answer: The right face numeral is the same, but points in different directions. The top and front numerals change values.

> *How can you tell that a cube has been tumbled left or right?*

Answer: The front face numeral stays the same, but points in different directions. The right and top numerals change values. Write the following rules on the chalkboard:

> FACE THAT KEEPS THE SAME NUMERAL
>> TOP: Turning right or left
>> RIGHT: Tumbling forward or backward
>> FRONT: Tumbling left or right

> *Look at the first three cubes. Which face keeps the same numeral?*

Answer: The right face.

> *Without looking at the rules, how is the cube changing position?*

Answer: Tumbling forward.

> *How do you know?*

Answer: First the **2** is on its back, then on its base, and then on its face.

> *If you were on your back, then upright, and then on your face, you would be tumbling forward. How will the cube look if it tumbles forward one more time?*

Answer: The **2** should be upside down on the right face. Cube **b** is marked that way and is the correct answer. If necessary, demonstrate the sequence using the paper cube.

Optional demonstration for ROTATING CUBES—DESCRIBE (pages 187–188):
If students have difficulty with **B-311**, use the following discussion:

> *Look at the EXAMPLE on page 187. Which face keeps the same numeral?*

Answer: The top face.

> *Is the cube rotating or tumbling?*

Answer: Rotating.

> *How can you tell which direction the cube is rotating?*

Answer: Since the **6** moves from the right face to the front face (or the direction the **3** is turning can serve as a clue), the cube is turning to the left.

Does the change between cubes B ***and*** C ***support the idea that the cube is rotating to the left?***
Answer: Yes; the **4** from the right face moved to the front and the **3** on top turned to its face.

Now look at question a. ***What number is on the back of cube*** A***? Use the idea that the cube is turning instead of your memory of the position of the various numbers.***
Answer: **4**. Since the cube is turning to the left, the right face of cube **B** is the same face that was hidden on the back of cube **A**.

Now look at question b. ***What number is on the left face of cube*** C***?***
Answer: **6**. Since the cube is turning to the left, the front face of cube **B** will be hidden on the left face of cube **C**.

Now look at question c. ***What number is on the back of cube*** B***?***
Answer: **1**. Since the cube is turning to the left, the right face of cube **C** is the face that was hidden on the back of cube **B**.

Optional demonstration for ROTATING CUBES—SUPPLY (pages 189–190):
If students have difficulty with **B-316**, use the following discussion:

In the EXAMPLE on page 189, which face keeps the same numeral?
Answer: The top face.

How is the cube moving?
Answer: Rotating to the left.

How do you know it is rotating to the left?
Answer: Because the face on the right always becomes the front face, e.g., the **2** on the right face of the first cube moves to the front face of the second cube (or the direction the **3** is turning can serve as a clue).

Look at the last cube. Why is the front face marked 4***?***
Answer: The cube is turning to the left so the **4** from the right face of the previous cube moves to the front.

Why is the right face marked 1***?***
Answer: The cube is turning to the left. As you look at the other cubes, you see that the **1**, which was on the front of the first cube, moves to the left face of the second cube, and then to the back face of the third cube. With one more turn, the **1** moves to the right face. (One can also look at the location of the numeral **1** in relation to the numeral **3**.)

GUIDED PRACTICE:
EXERCISE: **B-308**
Give students sufficient time to complete this exercise. Then, using the demonstration methodology above, have them discuss and explain their choice.
ANSWER: **B-308** c

DISCUSSION TIPS:
During discussion of answers, students should identify the face that changes direction without changing value, describe the type and direction of the cube's movement, and state reasons for eliminating the alternate answer choices. This activity may be extended by asking students to identify all faces of each answer cube.

INDEPENDENT PRACTICE:
Assign exercises **B-309** through **B-322**

ANSWERS:
B-309 a; **B-310** c
B-311 a 3, **b** 1, **c** 5; **B-312 a** 6, **b** 1, **c** 2; **B-313 a** 6, **b** 1, **c** 1; **B-314 a** 6, **b** 6, **c** 4;
B-315 a 1, **b** 5, **c** 6

B-316 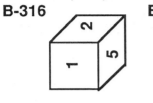   **B-317** 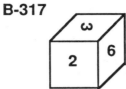   **B-318** 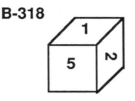   **B-319**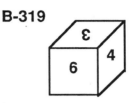

B-320 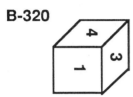   **B-321** 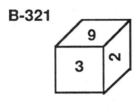   **B-322**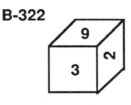

FOLLOW-UP REFERENT:
   When might you need to recognize the relative position of the sides of a cube?
Examples: model building; assembling cardboard file boxes, airline boxes for soft
luggage, or display racks; games involving dice; construction projects

CURRICULUM APPLICATION:
Language Arts: preparing and presenting descriptions of solid shapes or figures
Mathematics: position discrimination involving cubes and prisms
Science: observing and recognizing different views of organisms or geological features
Social Studies: recognizing relative positions on globes or other three-dimensional
   maps
Enrichment Areas: career education discussions involving architecture, engineering,
   construction, drafting, graphic design, and archaeology; design principles for molds
   and sculptures; drafting and architectural drawing; reading blueprints; industrial arts
   or art projects

EXTENDING ACTIVITIES:
None.

FIGURAL CLASSIFICATIONS

DESCRIBING CLASSES

STRAND: Figural Classifications   **PAGES:** 191–192

ADDITIONAL MATERIALS:
Transparency of student workbook page 191

INTRODUCTION:
In previous exercises you recognized similarities and differences among shapes and figures; arranged shapes, figures, and patterns into sequences; and identified common characteristics of shapes and figures.

OBJECTIVE:
In these exercises you will choose statements which describe the characteristics of all the shapes or figures in a given group or class.

DEMONSTRATION/EXPLANATION:
Project the **EXAMPLE** from the transparency of page 191, indicating each statement as you explain.
You are to determine which statements to the right are true of all the shapes or figures in the given class. Are all these shapes rectangles?
Answer: No; only two have right angles.
Are they all white?
Answer: Yes.
Are they all the same size?
Answer: No.
Do they all have four sides?
Answer: Yes.
How would you describe this class?
Answer: A group of white, four-sided shapes.

GUIDED PRACTICE:
EXERCISES: **C-1, C-2, C-3**
Give students sufficient time to complete these exercises. Then, using the demonstration methodology above, have them discuss and explain their choices.
ANSWERS: **C-1** a and c; **C-2** a, c, d, and e; **C-3** b and d

INDEPENDENT PRACTICE:
Assign exercises **C-4** through **C-7**

DISCUSSION TIPS:
This exercise promotes thoroughness in description and examination. The important word is **all**. **All** members of a class must have common characteristics or attributes. Since most of the given classes possess more than a single common attribute, students must

read each descriptive phrase, look at the class, and decide if the statement is true. During class discussion, ask students to explain why they believe a statement to be true or false. They should also be able to describe the class in a single sentence.

ANSWERS:
C-4 c and d; **C-5** b and d; **C-6** a, d, and e; **C-7** b and c

FOLLOW-UP REFERENT:
When might you be asked to identify characteristics of something you see?
Examples: field-trip observations; science experiments; reporting or giving statements regarding an accident, injury, or fire to the proper officials

CURRICULUM APPLICATION:
Language Arts: describing things or people; writing news articles; providing written or oral directions for constructions or travelling
Mathematics: describing geometric shapes
Science: classifying leaves, insects, flowers, shells, or birds based on appearance; describing characteristics of science experiments or demonstration results
Social Studies: interpreting charts and graphs; drawing inferences from pictures or artifacts; stating generalities that are true of a historic era, event, or people
Enrichment Areas: describing a work of art or a dance; applying statements of characteristics to creative works, eras, or "schools"

EXTENDING ACTIVITIES:
None.

MATCHING CLASSES

STRAND: Figural Classifications   **PAGES:** 193–194

ADDITIONAL MATERIALS:
Transparency of student workbook page 193
Washable transparency markers (five different colors)

INTRODUCTION:
In the previous exercise you identified statements which described all given members of a class.

OBJECTIVE:
In these exercises you will match groups having the same characteristics.

DEMONSTRATION/EXPLANATION:
Project the transparency of page 193. Use different colored markers to connect the correct answer choices as students respond.
How would you describe the shapes in the EXAMPLE.
Answer: All the shapes have three straight lines, one curved line, and two right angles.

Which group on the right matches this description?
Answer: **c**
   Describe the shapes in group C-8.
Answer: All the shapes have four straight lines and one curved line.
   Which group on the right contains shapes which belong in this class?
Answer: **d**
   Describe the shapes in group C-9.
Answer: All the shapes have seven straight lines.
   Which other group belongs in this class?
Answer: **a**

GUIDED PRACTICE:
EXERCISES: **C-10, C-11**
Give students sufficient time to complete these exercises. Then, using the demonstration methodology above, have them discuss and explain their choices.
ANSWERS: **C-10** e (two straight lines and two arcs); **C-11** b (six straight lines)

INDEPENDENT PRACTICE:
Assign exercises **C-12** through **C-16**

DISCUSSION TIPS:
Encourage students to use precise vocabulary when describing shape and pattern. Geometric terms, e.g., **right triangle**, **trapezoid**, etc., are encouraged if the words are already familiar to students. Imaginative similes, e.g., **arrowhead**, **home plate**, etc., are encouraged when nonconventional shapes are used.

ANSWERS:
C-12 d (one axis of symmetry); **C-13** e (no axis of symmetry); **C-14** a (three congruent parts); **C-15** b (two congruent parts); **C-16** c (two axes of symmetry)

FOLLOW-UP REFERENT:
   When might you be asked to match groups of objects according to their common characteristics?
Examples: sorting construction toys, eating utensils, clothing, or tools; reshelving or locating items in a store, warehouse, library, or workshop

CURRICULUM APPLICATION:
Language Arts: matching letter styles by placement and punctuation, e.g., business
   letters, friendly letters, memos
Mathematics: comparing numbers using place values; using arithmetic symbols to group
   like problems; grouping geometric shapes
Science: classifying by shape or pattern, e.g., leaves, insects, flowers, shells, birds;
   identifying symmetry and geometric forms found in the environment
Social Studies: examining pictures or artifacts for drawing inferences; finding the same
   location on different types or sizes of maps; using legends to read graphs, maps, charts
Enrichment Areas: locating types of books or items in a library; matching typefaces, or
   page designs in journalism; classifying musical instruments by tone, design, or shape,

e.g., winds, reeds, percussion; classifying works of art by medium; relating new knowledge to previous knowledge

EXTENDING ACTIVITIES:
None.

CLASSIFYING MORE THAN ONE WAY—MATCHING

STRAND: Figural Classifications   **PAGES:** 195–197

ADDITIONAL MATERIALS:
Transparency of student workbook page 195
Washable transparency marker

INTRODUCTION:
In previous exercises you described classes by common characteristics and matched classes with a common shape or pattern.

OBJECTIVE:
In these exercises you will decide how many ways you can classify a given shape or figure.

DEMONSTRATION/EXPLANATION:
Project the transparency of page 195.
Look at the EXAMPLE. The hexagon belongs in class f because all the shapes in that class are hexagons. It also belongs in classes b and e because all the shapes in those classes are white. How would you describe the figure in C-17?
Answer: A white circle divided into four equal parts by two intersecting diagonal lines.
Who can find a matching class in the lettered boxes to the right? Be sure you can tell why the figure can belong to that class.
Answers: Classes **a** (circles), **c**, and **f** (two intersecting lines in pattern).
Describe class b. Why can't figure C-17 belong in that class?
Answer: Class **b** consists of white (plain, no pattern) right triangles. Figure **C-17** is neither plain nor a right triangle.
Describe class d. Why can't figure C-17 belong in that class?
Answer: Class **d** consists of only shaded shapes. Figure **C-17** is not shaded.
Describe class e. Why can't figure C-17 belong in that class?
Answer: Class **e** consists of white (plain, no pattern) four-sided shapes with one or more pair of parallel sides. Figure **C-17** is not plain, not four-sided, and has no parallel sides.

GUIDED PRACTICE:
EXERCISES: **C-18, C-19, C-20**
Give students sufficient time to complete these exercises. Then, using the demonstration methodology above, have them discuss and explain their choices.
ANSWERS: **C-18** d (black) and e (four-sided); **C-19** a (half-black) and f (hexagons); **C-20** b (white right triangles) and e (white)

INDEPENDENT PRACTICE:
Assign exercises **C-21** through **C-37**

DISCUSSION TIPS:
Encourage students to explain why each shape or figure does or does not belong to each pictured class. Have students name the class each time.

ANSWERS:
C-21 a (circles), c, and f (intersecting lines within shape); **C-22** e (four-sided), c and f (intersecting lines within shape)

PAGE 196 CLASS IDENTIFICATIONS:
a. four axes of symmetry, squares, equilateral, equiangular, four-sided, four right angles
b. single axis of symmetry, diagonal axis of symmetry—northwest to southeast
c. two axes of symmetry, vertical and horizontal axes of symmetry
d. two axes of symmetry, diagonal axes—northeast–southwest and northwest–southeast
e. single axis of symmetry, diagonal axis of symmetry—northeast to southwest
f. single axis of symmetry, vertical axis of symmetry, two pair of equal angles
g. single axis of symmetry, horizontal axis of symmetry
C-23 best class–a, can also go in all other classes; **C-24** best class–g, can also go in b, e, and f; **C-25** best class–d, can also go in b, c, and e; **C-26** best class–f, can also go in b, c, e, and g; **C-27** best class–b, can also go in d, e, f, and g; **C-28** best class–a, can also go in all other classes; **C-29** best class–e, can also go in b, d, f, and g

PAGE 197 CLASS IDENTIFICATIONS:
a. circle within a shape
b. shape within a circle
c. triangle within a shape
d. shape within a triangle
e. square within a shape
f. shape within a parallelogram
C-30 f ; **C-31** d; **C-32** a; **C-33** a or f; **C-34** b; **C-35** c; **C-36** c or d; **C-37** e

FOLLOW-UP REFERENT:
When might you be asked to sort objects in more than one way?
Examples: sorting tools or materials for different projects; arranging items on shelves; arranging collections of objects, e.g., using country of origin, denomination, or date of issue to sort stamps or money

CURRICULUM APPLICATION:
Language Arts: changing sentence meanings using vocal inflections or different end marks; arranging groups of words into various categories, e.g., alphabetical order, initial letters, words that end in -ing
Mathematics: using the same numbers to create different problems; sorting geometric shapes and patterns
Science: classifying leaves, insects, flowers, shells, or birds using shape, pattern, or color; using matrices to classify items by shape, pattern, or color

Social Studies: making different types of charts or graphs illustrating results of a poll or other statistical information; grouping artifacts using various categories, e.g., material, use, design

Enrichment Areas: selecting proper material for an art project; classifying music using different categories, e.g., type, purpose, instrument, style, composer

EXTENDING ACTIVITIES:
None.

CHANGING CHARACTERISTICS—SELECT

STRAND: Figural Classifications   **PAGES:** 198–199

ADDITIONAL MATERIALS:
Transparency of student workbook page 198
Washable transparency marker

INTRODUCTION:
In previous exercises you classified according to shape or pattern and learned that the same object can belong to more than one class.

OBJECTIVE:
In these exercises you will identify which characteristics of a pair of figures are the same and which are different.

DEMONSTRATION/EXPLANATION:
Project the transparency of page 198.

Look at the EXAMPLE. Are these two shapes the same size?

Answer: No; the second one is smaller so the size is different.

Since they are not the same size, circle D (for different) in the Size row. Do they have the same shape?

Answer: Yes; both are right triangles with two equal sides.

Since they are the same shape, circle S (for same) in the Shape row. Do the two shapes have the same pattern or color?

Answer: No; the large triangle is white and the small triangle is black. Circle D in the Pattern row.

Do they face in the same direction?

Answer: No; the right angle on the right side of the larger triangle and on the left side of the smaller triangle. Circle D in the Direction row.

How would you describe a class that contained these two shapes?

Answer: A class of right isosceles triangles.

What other shapes could be included in the same class?

Answer: Any right triangle having two equal sides (isosceles), regardless of size, pattern, or direction. If time allows, have several students draw additional shapes on the chalkboard for class discussion.

GUIDED PRACTICE:
EXERCISES: C-38, C-39
Give students sufficient time to complete these exercises. Then, using the demonstration methodology above, have them discuss and explain their choices.
ANSWERS:
C-38 Size: D, Shape: D, Pattern: S (Class: any half-black symmetrical figure, regardless of size or shape)
C-39 Size: S, Shape: S, Pattern: S, Direction: D (Class: any hexagon with the same size and pattern, regardless of direction)

INDEPENDENT PRACTICE:
Assign exercises **C-40** through **C-44**

DISCUSSION TIPS:
Encourage students to explain how the pairs of figures are different.

ANSWERS:
C-40 Size: D, Shape: D, Pattern: D (if color and size are criteria) **or** S (if pattern is defined as repeating the shape in the opposite color) (Class: similar shape within shape, colored opposite)
C-41 Size: D, Shape: S, Pattern: D, Direction: D (Class: any triangle)
C-42 Size: D, Shape: D, Pattern: S, Direction: D (Class: half-black symmetrical shapes)
C-43 Size: D, Shape: S, Pattern: D (the intersecting lines in one start at the corners, while the other is divided at the end point of the sides) **or** S (if pattern is seen as intersecting sloping perpendicular lines), Direction: D (Class: squares with pattern of intersecting perpendicular lines)
C-44 Size: D, Shape: S, Pattern: D (considering color) **or** S (considering shapes shaded opposite) (Class: circle within circle, shaded opposite)

FOLLOW-UP REFERENT:
When might you be asked to identify changing characteristics?
Examples: choosing correct tools, utensils, or materials for a project; differentiating among similar, but not identical, objects

CURRICULUM APPLICATION:
Language Arts: differentiating between proper and common nouns or adjectives; identifying singular, plural, and possessive forms of words
Mathematics: observing how increasing the value of a variable in a formula changes the answer given by the formula, e.g., what happens to the area of a square when the sides are doubled; reading graphs; rotation, reflection, similarity, and congruence exercises; differentiating among specialized geometric shapes, e.g., quadrilaterals: squares, rectangles, rhombuses, trapezoids
Science: identifying seasonal or growth changes in living things; observing life cycles of living organisms; describing changes in cloud formations; observing changes in different elements on the earth, e.g., soil erosion or caking, physical changes caused by forest fires; describing changes in science experiments
Social Studies: observing historical changes in artifacts, architectural styles, dress, and social, political, or judicial systems

Enrichment Areas: observing historical changes in art, music, dance, furniture, clothing, or entertainment; observing changes in an artist's style over time

EXTENDING ACTIVITIES:
None.

DESCRIBING CHARACTERISTICS

STRAND: Figural Classifications   **PAGES:** 200–201

ADDITIONAL MATERIALS:
Transparency of student workbook page 200
Washable transparency marker

INTRODUCTION:
In the previous exercise you identified similar and different characteristics of two given figures.

OBJECTIVE:
In these exercises you will identify and describe how characteristics of shapes are the same and how they are different.

DEMONSTRATION/EXPLANATION:
Project the **EXAMPLE** from the transparency of page 200, covering the answers.
Remember the kinds of characteristics you considered when comparing and contrasting two objects? How are these two shapes different?
Pause for student responses. Possible answers: The square is taller, has a different number of sides, and different angles.
How are they alike?
Possible answers: Each is equilateral and equiangular; the bases are the same length; the shapes are the same color. It may be necessary to use direct questioning to get the students to arrive at these multiple answers.
How would you describe a class that included both shapes?
Answer: A class of white, equilateral, equiangular shapes with a one-inch base.

GUIDED PRACTICE:
EXERCISE: **C-45**
Give students sufficient time to complete this exercise. Then, using the demonstration methodology above, have them discuss and explain their choices.
ANSWER: **C-45** Alike: four sides, opposite sides parallel, same height
              Different: only the rectangle is equiangular, different base

INDEPENDENT PRACTICE:
Assign exercises **C-46** through **C-49**

DISCUSSION TIPS:
Encourage students to look for detailed similarities and differences between the shapes they are comparing. They should be able to state the characteristics of each class in a

single sentence. To extend this activity, ask students to describe a shape that could **not** fit in the class.

ANSWERS:

C-46 Alike: both are equilateral
Different: number of sides, different height and base, only the triangle is equiangular
C-47 Alike: four sides, four right angles, same size base, opposite sides parallel
Different: height, only the square is equilateral
C-48 Alike: equilateral, opposite sides parallel
Different: number of sides, only the hexagon is equiangular
C-49 Alike: four sides, same size base, same height, opposite sides parallel
Different: only the square is equiangular

FOLLOW-UP REFERENT:
When might you be asked to identify how two things are similar and different?
Examples: field-trip observations; science experiments; geometry exercises

CURRICULUM APPLICATION:
Language Arts: describing changing phenomena
Mathematics: observing how increasing the value of a variable in a formula changes the answer given by the formula, e.g., what happens to the area of a square when the lengths of its sides are doubled
Science: identifying seasonal or growth changes in living things, e.g., leaves, insects, flowers, shells, birds; observing changes in rocks produced by weathering
Social Studies: examining pictures of artifacts for drawing inferences in social studies; observing historical changes in customs, national purpose, language
Enrichment Areas: observing historical changes in art, music, or entertainment

EXTENDING ACTIVITIES:
None.

CHANGING CHARACTERISTICS—SUPPLY

STRAND: Figural Classifications   **PAGES:** 202–203

ADDITIONAL MATERIALS:
Transparency of student workbook page 202
Washable transparency marker

INTRODUCTION:
In the previous exercise you identified and described how the characteristics of two shapes were similar and different.

OBJECTIVE:
In these exercises you will draw a figure using characteristics described in the directions.

DEMONSTRATION/EXPLANATION:

Project the **EXAMPLE** from the transparency of page 202, covering the directions and the answer.

> *How would you describe this figure?*

Answer: A white square with one-inch sides and a wide, vertical, black stripe connecting the centers of the top and bottom sides. Project the **DIRECTIONS**.

> *Read these directions, then describe the resulting figure.*

Answer: The figure will be a white square with less than one-inch sides and a wide, vertical, black stripe connecting the top and bottom sides. Project the **ANSWER** and ask students to confirm that the figure conforms to the Directions. Project exercise **C-50**.

> *Describe the figure that will result from following the Directions in exercise C-50.*

Answer: The figure will be a larger black circle with a wide, white, vertical stripe. Have a student draw the **ANSWER** figure on the transparency, then confirm the drawing by checking it against the Directions. Answer:

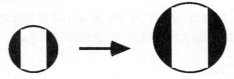

GUIDED PRACTICE:

EXERCISE: **C-51**

Give students sufficient time to complete this exercise. Then, using the demonstration methodology above, have them discuss and explain their choice.

ANSWER:

C-51

INDEPENDENT PRACTICE:

Assign exercises **C-52** through **C-56**

DISCUSSION TIPS:

Encourage students to be specific regarding size, shape, pattern, and direction when describing the figures in each pair.

ANSWERS:

C-52   C-53   C-54

C-55   C-56

FOLLOW-UP REFERENT:
> *When might you be asked to produce or draw an object with certain characteristics changed?*

Examples: field trip observations; science experiments; geometry exercises

CURRICULUM APPLICATION:
Language Arts: writing descriptions of changing phenomena
Mathematics: illustrating how a change in the value of a variable changes the answer given by the formula, e.g., what happens to the area of a square when the lengths of the sides are doubled
Science: illustrating seasonal or growth changes in living things, e.g., leaves, insects, flowers, shells, birds; illustrating changes in rocks produced by weathering
Social Studies: examining pictures of artifacts for drawing inferences in social studies; illustrating historical changes in customs, national purpose, language
Enrichment Areas: illustrating examples of historical changes in art, music, or entertainment

EXTENDING ACTIVITIES:
None.

DRAW ANOTHER

STRAND: Figural Classifications   **PAGES:** 204–207

ADDITIONAL MATERIALS:
Transparency of student workbook page 204
Washable transparency marker

INTRODUCTION:
> *In previous exercises you identified and formed classes of shapes and figures.*

OBJECTIVE:
> *In these exercises you will determine the common characteristics of a class, then supply another shape or figure that can belong to that class.*

DEMONSTRATION/EXPLANATION:
Project the transparency of page 204.
> *In exercise C-57, what are the characteristics of the class?*

Answer: Shape: right triangle; Pattern: connecting midpoints of two sides, with one of the sections shaded.
> *Who can draw another figure that could fit in this class?*

Student should draw other figures using the grid on the transparency. Answer: Any right triangle divided by connecting the midpoints of two sides and shading one portion. Ask the class to confirm that the supplied figures fit the class. For example:

Project exercise **C-58**.
What are the characteristics of this class?
Answer: Shape: symmetrical pentagon with two right angles and two pair of equal sides;
Pattern: half-black.
Who will draw another figure that could fit in this class?
Confirm students' drawing. Answer: Any half-black symmetrical pentagon containing two
right angles, two pair of equal sides, and a line of symmetry connecting the apex to the
midpoint of the base. For example:

GUIDED PRACTICE:
EXERCISE: **C-59**
Give students sufficient time to complete this exercise. Then, using the demonstration
methodology above, have them discuss and explain their choice. Have students name
the class each time.
ANSWER:

C-59   Draw any three sides of a square
or rectangle, then draw in the diagonals
connecting the corners. Shade the
triangle opposite the open side.

INDEPENDENT PRACTICE:
Assign exercises **C-60** through **C-69**

DISCUSSION TIPS:
Students should accurately describe the shape and pattern of each class.

ANSWERS:
C-60   **C-61**   **C-62**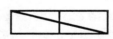

Draw any parallelogram, then
connect the opposite midpoints
with straight lines.

Draw a rectangle. Extend the
two shorter sides in the same
direction to different lengths.
Draw a line connecting the
endpoints of the extensions.

Draw any rectangle with the long
dimension east-west. Draw the
diagonal connecting the northwest
corner and the southeast corner.
Draw a line connecting the midpoints
of the top and the base.

C-63

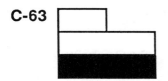

Draw two congruent rectangles joined along their long sides. Drawanother rectangle the same width but half the length of the first two rectangles. Join it by its longer side to one of the larger rectangles, making an L-shaped figure. Shade the rectangle furthest from the small rectangle.

C-64

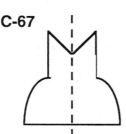

Draw a square within a square so the sides are parallel and and equal border remains around the inner one. Shade one of the squares.

C-65

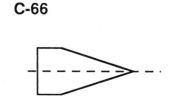

Draw any tetrominoe (see workbook page 75). Shade alternate squares.

C-66

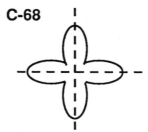

Draw any figure having a horizontal line of symmetry.

C-67

Draw any figure having a vertical line of symmetry.

C-68

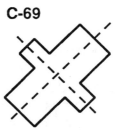

Draw any figure having both horizontal and vertical lines of symmetry.

C-69

Draw any figure having diagonal lines of symmetry.

FOLLOW-UP REFERENT:

When are you asked to determine a class, then provide another member?
Examples: reshelving books in a library; locating substitute parts for models, motors, or gears; locating objects that illustrate specific geometric shapes

CURRICULUM APPLICATION:

Language Arts: adding words to given lists when the category depends on word configuration rather than meaning, e.g., -ing words, -ance words, doubled consonant words; identifying punctuation and proofreading marks
Mathematics: adding numbers or shapes to given sets; constructing geometric shapes
Science: naming items that could be classified together; identifying cloud formations
Social Studies: naming states by geographic region or other given category; using an atlas to find regions sharing particular attributes; adding additional information to an existing chart or graph
Enrichment Areas: creating different art projects using the same type of material; adding to lists of instrument types, e.g., percussion, woodwinds, brass, strings

EXTENDING ACTIVITIES:

None.

CLASSIFYING BY SHAPE/PATTERN—SORTING

STRAND: Figural Classifications   **PAGES:** 208–215

ADDITIONAL MATERIALS:
Transparency of student workbook page 208 (cut out the top figures)

INTRODUCTION:
In previous exercises you described and identified classes and matched shapes or figures according to common characteristics.

OBJECTIVE:
In these exercises you will sort all the given shapes or figures into classes.

DEMONSTRATION/EXPLANATION:
Project exercise **C-70** from the transparency of page 208, placing the cutout pieces as they appear in the exercise.
This exercise concerns sorting figures by pattern. Each figure will belong in one of the classes shown here.
Point to the boxes with the patterned hexagon headings. Indicate shape **1**.
How would you describe the pattern of this figure?
Answer: One vertical and one horizontal line intersecting at the midpoints.
Which of these four classes has a similar pattern?
Answer: The first column. Place figure **1** inside the correct class box, then indicate figure **12**.
How would you describe the pattern of this figure?
Answer: Two diagonal lines intersecting at the midpoints.
To which class does it belong?
Answer: The second column. Place figure **12** in the correct class box.

GUIDED PRACTICE:
EXERCISE: remainder of **C-70**
Give students sufficient time to complete this exercise. Then, using the demonstration methodology above, have them discuss and explain their choices.
ANSWER:

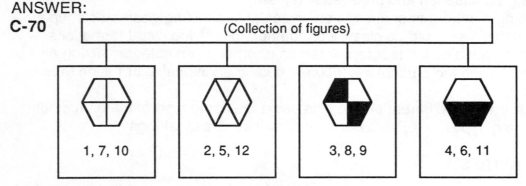

C-70

INDEPENDENT PRACTICE:
Assign exercises **C-71** through **C-77.** Remind students that they must classify **all** shapes or figures given in each exercise.

DISCUSSION TIPS:

Students should use precise vocabulary and geometric terms when describing shape and pattern. Encourage imaginative similes, e.g., **arrowhead**, **home plate**, when referring to nonconventional shapes. In exercises **C-76** and **C-77**, correct answers depend on correct shape placement according to the classification criteria chosen, rather than correct criteria selection. Remind students that **all** given shapes must be classified in each exercise.

ANSWERS:
C-71

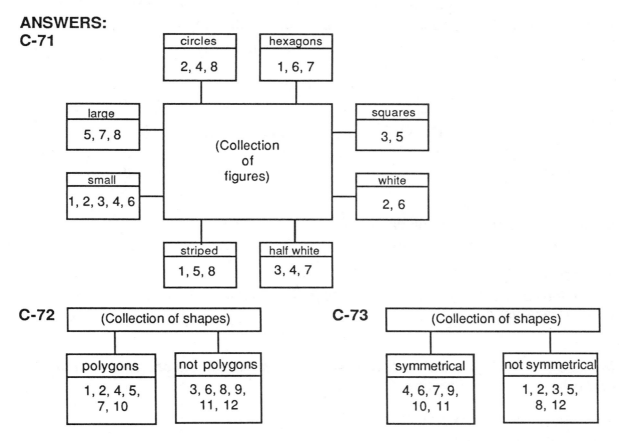

C-74, C-75, C-76

Answers will vary according to the chosen sorting characteristics. Possible classes and subclasses include:

     –symmetrical and not symmetrical
     –polygons and not plygons
     –curved lines and straight lines
     –parallel lines and no parallel lines

FOLLOW-UP REFERENT:

    When might you need to determine classes and sort objects in different ways?
Examples: sorting toys, utensils, tools, books, or supplies; sorting items into boxes for moving or packing away

CURRICULUM APPLICATION:

Language Arts: grouping lists of words according to criteria based upon word
   configuration rather than meaning, e.g., -ing words, -ance words, initial letter

Mathematics: grouping random numbers into given sets; adding or subtracting multiple digit numbers by regrouping; placing numeric information onto charts or graphs

Science: classifying objects or items into given categories when all subjects must be classified; classifying days of the week or month according to given weather parameters, e.g., temperature, fog, rain, snow

Social Studies: placing events or dates on a predetermined time line; determining what information to use and how to arrange it on a chart, map, or graph

Enrichment Areas: classifying crayons, paints, or markers according to color family or other category; classifying music or art media according to categories

EXTENDING ACTIVITIES:
None.

OVERLAPPING CLASSES—INTERSECTIONS

STRAND: Figural Classifications   **PAGES:** 216–225

ADDITIONAL MATERIALS:
Transparency of student workbook page 216
Washable transparency markers (three colors)

INTRODUCTION:
In previous exercises you sorted shapes and figures according to more than one characteristic.

OBJECTIVE:
In these exercises you will sort some shapes or figures using one characteristic and others by more than one characteristic.

DEMONSTRATION/EXPLANATION:
Project the transparency of page 216.

Look at the Venn (overlapping classes) *diagram. This diagram contains four areas—circle A, circle B, the intersection of circles A and B, and outside circles A and B. What type of shape would fit in circle A?*

Trace circle **A** using a colored transparency markers. Answer: Black shapes.

What shapes go in the class for circle B?

Trace circle **B** using a second colored marker. Answer: Regular polygons.

What letter marks the intersection of these two circles and what type of shapes would fit in this intersection?

Trace the outline of the intersection using a third colored marker. Answer: The letter **I**; black, regular polygons.

What kinds of shapes would go in class O—outside circles A and B?

Answer: Any irregular shape or nonpolygon that is not black, i.e., white circles, half-black rectangles.

Why does the white triangle shown in the EXAMPLE belong in circle B?

Answer: It is a regular polygon (all sides are equal) and it is not black.
> **Where does the shape in C-78 belong?**

Answer: Circle **A**.
> **Why can't it go in circle B?**

Answer: It is not a regular polygon. Write an <u>A</u> in the answer blank for exercise **C-78**.
> **In what region does the shape in C-79 belong?**

Answer: Region O—outside the circles.
> **Why doesn't it go in circles A or B?**

Answer: It is not black, so it cannot go in circle **A**, and it does not have equal sides, so it cannot go in circle **B**. Write an <u>O</u> in the answer blank.
> **In which region does the shape in C-80 belong?**

Answer: Region **I**, the intersection of circles **A** and **B**.
> **Why does it belong in this region?**

Answer: It can fit in circle **A** because it is black and circle **B** because all of its sides are equal. Write an <u>I</u> in the answer blank.

GUIDED PRACTICE:
EXERCISES: **C-81, C-82, C-83, C-84, C-85**
Give students sufficient time to complete these exercises. Then, using the demonstration methodology above, have them discuss and explain their choices.
ANSWERS: **C-81** B; **C-82** O; **C-83** A; **C-84** B; **C-85** I

INDEPENDENT PRACTICE:
Assign exercises **C-86** through **C-159**

DISCUSSION TIPS:
On pages 222 and 223 students must observe and determine the characteristics of each class. It is important that students explain why a given shape of figure cannot fit into any other region of the diagram.

ANSWERS:
C-86 triangles; **C-87** black shapes; **C-88** black triangles; **C-89** B; **C-90** O; **C-91** A;
C-92 B; **C-93** O; **C-94** I

C-95 striped shapes; **C-96** triangles; **C-97** B; **C-98** A; **C-99** B; **C-100** O; **C-101** I;
C-102 A

C-103 I; **C-104** O; **C-105** A; **C-106** B; **C-107** A; **C-108** I

| C-109 | C-110 | C-111 | C-112 | C-113 |

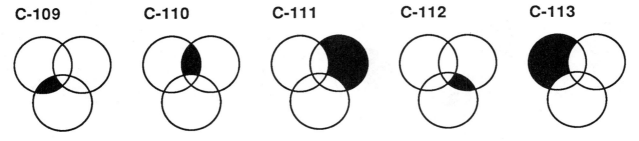

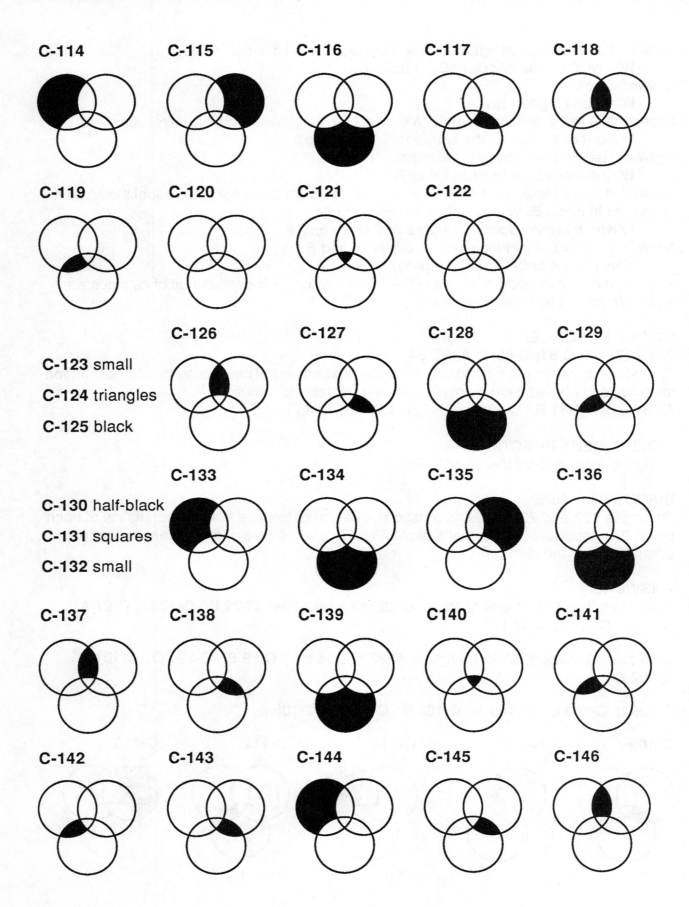

C-114   C-115   C-116   C-117   C-118

C-119   C-120   C-121   C-122

C-123 small
C-124 triangles
C-125 black

C-126   C-127   C-128   C-129

C-130 half-black
C-131 squares
C-132 small

C-133   C-134   C-135   C-136

C-137   C-138   C-139   C140   C-141

C-142   C-143   C-144   C-145   C-146

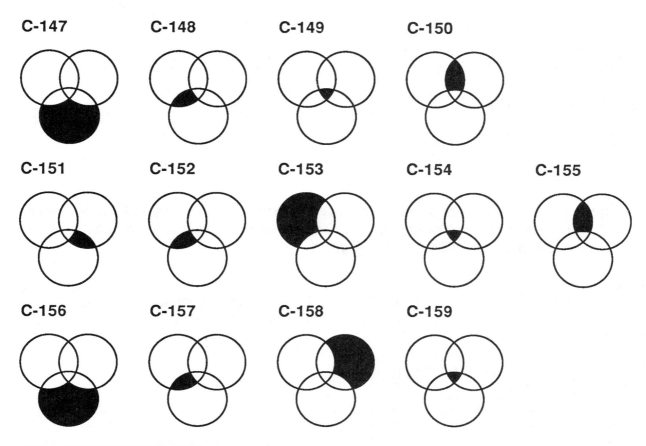

C-147 C-148 C-149 C-150

C-151 C-152 C-153 C-154 C-155

C-156 C-157 C-158 C-159

FOLLOW-UP REFERENT:
When might you need to sort objects into classes, some of which might overlap?
Examples: finding books or materials in a library; locating products in a grocery store; different uses for tools or materials, e.g., using one side of a claw hammer to drive in nails and the other side to pull them out

CURRICULUM APPLICATION:
Language Arts: classifying words into various categories based on word configuration rather than meaning, e.g., double consonant words, -ie words, -ance words; choosing appropriate illustrations for an original story or book
Mathematics: set theory exercises; attribute block exercises; sorting geometric shapes
Science: sorting natural objects into overlapping classes; indexing days according to different weather parameters, e.g., morning rain, afternoon rain, night rain, all-day rain
Social Studies: interpreting graphic information; using a legend to read a map; understanding the concept of classes and subclasses
Enrichment Areas: classifying musical instruments into different types, e.g., marching band/orchestra, jazz/rock; classifying works of art into different categories, e.g., era, medium, gender of artist

EXTENDING ACTIVITIES:
None.

OVERLAPPING CLASSES—MATRIX

STRAND: Figural Classifications   **PAGES:** 226–228

ADDITIONAL MATERIALS:
Transparency of student workbook page 226
Washable transparency marker
Attribute blocks (optional)

INTRODUCTION:
In the previous exercise some of the given shapes or figures could be classified by more than one characteristic. The overlapping circles diagram used to illustrate that relationship is called a Venn diagram.

OBJECTIVE:
In these exercises all the given shapes and figures are classified by more than one characteristic. To illustrate these relationships you will use a diagram called a matrix.

DEMONSTRATION/EXPLANATION:
<u>Optional demonstration using blocks</u>:
Draw a nine-cell matrix on the floor or sidewalk with chalk, or on a piece of cardboard with either chalk or a marker. Label the rows and columns as follows, placing the indicated attribute blocks in their corresponding cells. As you draw the matrix, explain which are rows and which are columns.

	SQUARES	CIRCLES	TRIANGLES
RED	RED		
YELLOW		YELLOW	
BLUE		BLUE	BLUE

What shape belongs in the top middle (Row 1, Column 2) ***cell?***
Answer: A red circle. By asking similar questions, lead students to complete the matrix.
NOTE: An alternate method might be to assign "cell values" to various students, then ask

*the class to place them on a floor matrix. For example: (*Student's name*), you are a blue square. Hand student a blue square shape to hold. Where should you be on this matrix? Students should be specific as to location of correct cell, naming it by row and column. After students respond, have the student holding the blue square stand in or place the object in the indicated cell until all students with "cell values" have been placed and the matrix is complete.*

<u>Demonstration using transparency</u>:
Project exercise **C-161** from the transparency of page 226.
> *Here is a matrix like the one you just finished, except the rows and columns have not been named. Which row has two figures drawn in?*

Answer: Row 3.
> *What do the two figures in Row 3 have in common?*

Answer: They are squares (shape).
> *Which column has two figures drawn in?*

Answer: Column 1.
> *What do the figures in Column 1 have in common?*

Answer: They have a horizontal midline (pattern).
> *It seems that in this matrix the figures in each row will have a common shape and the figures in each column will have a common pattern. That's shape for rows and pattern for columns. If this is true, what figure should be drawn in the Row 3, Column 1 cell?*

Answer: A square with a horizontal midline. Draw it in.
> *What figure should be drawn in the Row 1, Column 2 cell?*

Answer: A hexagon with a vertical midline. Draw it in.
> *What figure should be drawn in the Row 1, Column 3 cell?*

Answer: A hexagon with an X. Draw it in.
> *Now fill in the rest of the matrix.*

Confirm by discussion that students have drawn a circle with a vertical midline in Row 2, Column 2, and a circle with an X in Row 2, Column 3. Answer:

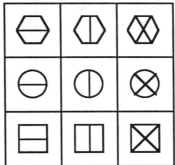

GUIDED PRACTICE:
EXERCISE: **C-160**
Give students sufficient time to complete this exercise. Then, using the demonstration methodology above, have them discuss and explain their choices.

ANSWERS:
C-160

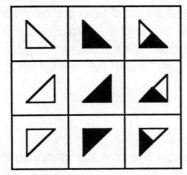

INDEPENDENT PRACTICE:
Assign exercises **C-162** through **C-165**

DISCUSSION TIPS:
Encourage students to use precise vocabulary when describing shape and pattern and to name the column and row characteristics.

ANSWERS:
C-162

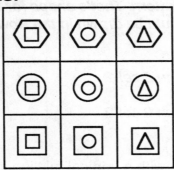

C-163

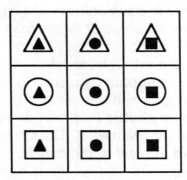

C-164

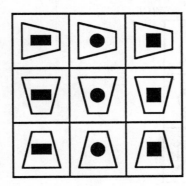

C-165

FOLLOW-UP REFERENT:
When might you need to read, construct, or complete a matrix?
Examples: using or making charts and class schedules

CURRICULUM APPLICATION:
Language Arts: locating information on graphs, tables, or schedules; comparing or contrasting elements in a story, passage, or play; charting characteristics of two characters in a story or play
Mathematics: reading addition, subtraction, or multiplication tables; creating or reading probability charts
Science: classifying using more than one characteristic; using tables or charts, e.g., periodic table, probability chart
Social Studies: making a graph or chart of survey results; using matrices to depict data
Enrichment Areas: using mileage matrices on road maps; comparing or contrasting works of art or pieces of music using multiple categories; comparing or contrasting works of two artists or composers

EXTENDING ACTIVITIES:
Building Thinking Skills, Book 3—Verbal, pp. 271–273

DEDUCE THE CLASS

STRAND: Figural Classifications   **PAGES:** 229–232

ADDITIONAL MATERIALS:
Transparency of student workbook page 230
Washable transparency marker

INTRODUCTION:
In previous exercises you classified shapes and figures by many different characteristics and learned how to name classes.

OBJECTIVE:
In these exercises you are given a made-up name for a class and several additional choices, some of which belong to the class and some of which do not. You are to determine the characteristics of the given class, then decide whether or not each additional shape or figure belongs to the class.

DEMONSTRATION/EXPLANATION:
Project the transparency of page 230. Point to the figures in the top left box.
    The figures in this box are all bitris. What do all these figures have in common?
Answer: Each is a closed figure made up of two triangles sharing a common side. Point to the figures in the top right box.
    None of the items pictured in this box are bitris. Why not?
Answer: None of the figures are made up of two triangles. Point to the **EXAMPLE**.
    Why is this a bitri?
Answer: It is a closed figure made up of two triangles having a common side (or because it looks a lot like one of the example bitris). Point to exercise **C-166**.
    Is this a bitri? Explain your answer.

Answer: No; it is a closed figure containing only one triangle. Write <u>NO</u> in the answer blank. Point to **C-167**.

> ***Is this a bitri? Explain your answer.***

Answer: No; it is a closed figure containing only one triangle. Write <u>NO</u> in the answer blank. Point to **C-168**.

> ***Is this a bitri? Explain your answer.***

Answer: Yes; because it is made up of two triangles sharing a common side, it is a bitri. Write <u>YES</u> in the answer blank.

GUIDED PRACTICE:
EXERCISES: **C-169, C-170**
Give students sufficient time to complete these exercises. Then, using the demonstration methodology above, have them discuss and explain their choices.
ANSWERS: **C-169** yes; **C-170** no

INDEPENDENT PRACTICE:
Assign exercises **C-171** through **C-182**

DISCUSSION TIPS:
When students have had sufficient time to do these exercises, discuss their answers using the same pattern of questioning. Students should explain why each figure is or is not a member of the class, confirming with each response the characteristic of the class.

ANSWERS:
C-171 no; **C-172** yes; **C-173** yes; **C-174** no; **C-175** yes; **C-176** no
C-177 yes; **C-178** no; **C-179** no; **C-180** yes; **C-181** no; **C-182** no

FOLLOW-UP REFERENT:
> ***When might you need to determine the characteristics of a class from given examples?***

Examples: examining evidence of any kind; utilizing inquiry methods in learning science or social studies

CURRICULUM APPLICATION:
Language Arts: inferring the layout of newspapers, books, or magazines from the format
   of similar items
Mathematics: classifying geometric shapes and irregular polygons
Science: describing given classes of plants or animals
Social Studies: making deductions about geographical features using given information;
   using prior knowledge to identify the culture to which artifacts belong
Enrichment Areas: using prior knowledge to classify or modify new information

EXTENDING ACTIVITIES:
Building Thinking Skills, Book 3–Verbal, pp. 115–122

FIGURAL ANALOGIES

FIGURAL ANALOGIES—SELECT

STRAND: Figural Analogies   **PAGES:** 233–237

ADDITIONAL MATERIALS:
Transparency of TM #28
Student handouts of TM #28
Washable transparency marker
Transparency of student workbook page 233 (optional)

INTRODUCTION:
In previous exercises you determined how shapes and figures were alike and different, put them in sequences, and separated them into classes.

OBJECTIVE:
In these exercises you will determine how two pairs of shapes or figures are related. That relationship is called an analogy.

DEMONSTRATION/EXPLANATION:
Optional demonstration using transparency of page 233:
If students are not familiar with the concept of an analogy, project the **EXAMPLE** from the transparency of page 233. Discuss the **EXAMPLE** with students. Encourage them to state the relationship between each pair and to explain why the other three answer choices are not related to the third shape in the same way the first two shapes are related.
Demonstration using TM #28:
Project transparency and distribute student handouts of TM #28.
In these sample exercises you have eight figures from which to make your answer choice. How would you read the partial analogy in exercise 1?
Answer: "A large white circle is to a small black circle as a large white square is to what?'
What would you do to the first shape to produce the second shape?
Answer: Reduce size and color opposite.
Remembering that the third and fourth shapes must show the same relationship, which answer in the CHOICE BOX will best complete the analogy?
Answer: **c**; a small black square.
Now look at exercise 2, read the analogy, and ask yourself the same question: "What would you do to the first figure to produce the second one?"
Answer: Reduce the width of the first figure by half.
Which answer in the CHOICE BOX will best complete the analogy?
Answer: **a**; the white square. Repeat this line of questioning for the remainder of TM #28 (or have students complete it as a **GUIDED PRACTICE** exercise). Answers: **3** d (reflect about the vertical); **4** b (rotate one position clockwise); **5** c (subtract detail–half the number of parts); **6** e (reflect about the horizontal); **7** f (duplicate the shape, rotate the duplicate two quarter-turns clockwise, join it to the original shape, and color it opposite)

GUIDED PRACTICE:
EXERCISES: **D-1, D-2**

Give students sufficient time to complete these exercises. Then, using the demonstration methodology above, have them discuss and explain their choices. Be sure students can explain why the alternate answer choices were eliminated.
ANSWERS: **D-1** b (reflect about the diagonal); **D-2** c (reflect about the vertical)

INDEPENDENT PRACTICE:
Assign exercises **D-3** through **D-20**

DISCUSSION TIPS:
Encourage students to use precise vocabulary when describing the figures. It may be helpful to review the types of figural changes introduced in the **FIGURAL SEQUENCES** section or review the relationships presented on student workbook page 241.

ANSWERS:
D-3 c (reduce size and color opposite); **D-4** a (reflect about the horizontal); **D-5** c (reflect about the vertical and color opposite)

D-6 h (increase size); **D-7** c (reflect about the \ diagonal); **D-8** g (color opposite); **D-9** a (rotate one quarter-turn clockwise)

D-10 g (color opposite and increase size); **D-11** e (reduce size and rotate one quarter-turn counterclockwise); **D-12** c (increase size and reflect about the / diagonal); **D-13** i (color opposite and decrease size); **D-14** h (increase size and reflect about the \ diagonal)

D-15 a (reflect about the horizontal); **D-16** a (reflect about the \ diagonal); **D-17** b (color opposite); **D-18** a (rotate one quarter-turn counterclockwise); **D-19** b (rotate one quarter-turn clockwise and color opposite); **D-20** e (reflect about the \ diagonal)

FOLLOW-UP REFERENT:
When might you need to recognize how two pairs of things are related?
Examples: matching articles of clothing and accessories; foreseeing consequences of moves in chess, checkers, or other games; comparing new information to previously known information; test-taking skills; arranging containers or dishes on shelves

CURRICULUM APPLICATION:
Language Arts: comparing or contrasting pictorial or graphic information
Mathematics: creating charts or graphs from numeric information; comparing or
    contrasting angles or polygons
Science: recognizing the relationship of cloud formations and weather; recognizing
    analogous body parts or structural elements in different organisms
Social Studies: recognizing parallel structures of governments, e.g., local to state to
    federal, monarchy to federalist; recognizing similar patterns in artifacts or in styles of
    architecture; comparing and/or contrasting information from maps, charts, or graphs
Enrichment Areas: test-taking skills; comparing and/or contrasting two types of music,
    art, or dance

EXTENDING ACTIVITIES:
None.

FIGURAL ANALOGIES—SELECT A PAIR/DESCRIBE

STRAND: Figural Analogies   **PAGES:** 238–242

ADDITIONAL MATERIALS:
Transparency of student workbook page 238
Washable transparency marker

INTRODUCTION:
In the previous exercise you selected a shape or figure which best completed an analogy.

OBJECTIVE:
In these exercises you will complete analogies by selecting a pair of figures. If "A is to B as C is to D," remember that C must be related to D in the same way that A is related to B.

DEMONSTRATION/EXPLANATION:
Project the transparency of page 238.
What is the relationship between the two figures in exercise D-21? What would you do to figure A to produce figure B?
Answer: Reflect about the vertical.
Which pair of figures in the C : D column shows the same change?
Answer: **c**
How are figures A and B related in exercise D-22?
Answer: Figure **A** has been reflected about the horizontal.
Which pair of figures in the C : D column shows a reflection about the horizontal?
Answer: **a**

GUIDED PRACTICE:
EXERCISES: **D-23, D-24, D-25**
Give students sufficient time to complete these exercises. Then, using the demonstration methodology above, have them discuss and explain their choices.
ANSWERS: **D-23** d (rotate one-quarter turn counterclockwise); **D-24** e (reflect about the / diagonal); **D-25** b (reflect about the \ diagonal)

INDEPENDENT PRACTICE:
Assign exercises **D-26** through **D-35**
NOTE: Remind students to complete page 242 by naming the types of analogy.

DISCUSSION TIPS:
As students state and discuss their choices, be sure they also describe the analogy type.

ANSWERS:
D-26 c (rotate one quarter-turn counterclockwise and color opposite); **D-27** e (reflect about the vertical and color opposite); **D-28** a (reflect about the horizontal and color opposite); **D-29** b (rotate one quarter-turn clockwise); **D-30** d (reflect about the vertical);

D-31 c (decrease size and color opposite); **D-32** e (reduce detail—halve the number of parts); **D-33** d (increase detail—double number of parts); **D-34** a (increase size and reflect about the \ diagonal); **D-35** b (increase size and reflect about the / diagonal)

FOLLOW-UP REFERENT:
When might you need to recognize how pairs of things are related?
Examples: matching articles of clothing and accessories; foreseeing consequences of moves in chess, checkers, or other games; comparing new information to previously known information; test-taking skills; arranging containers or dishes on shelves

CURRICULUM APPLICATION:
Language Arts: comparing or contrasting pictorial or graphic information
Mathematics: creating charts or graphs from numeric information; comparing or
    contrasting angles or polygons
Science: recognizing the relationship of cloud formations and weather; recognizing
    analogous body parts or structural elements in different organisms
Social Studies: recognizing parallel structures of governments, e.g., local to state to
    federal, monarchy to federalist; recognizing similar patterns in artifacts or in styles of
    architecture; comparing and/or contrasting information from maps, charts, or graphs
Enrichment Areas: test-taking skills; comparing and/or contrasting two types of music,
    art, or dance

EXTENDING ACTIVITIES:
None.

FIGURAL ANALOGIES—COMPLETE/SUPPLY

STRAND: Figural Analogies   **PAGES:** 243–247

ADDITIONAL MATERIALS:
Transparencies of student workbook pages 243 and 245
Washable transparency marker

INTRODUCTION:
In previous exercises you selected answers to best complete analogies.

OBJECTIVE:
In these exercises you will complete analogies by drawing the next figure.

DEMONSTRATION/EXPLANATION:
Project the **EXAMPLE** and exercise **D-36** from the transparency of page 243.
You are to draw a figure which shows the given relationship to the first figure according to the instructions for each exercise. The EXAMPLE shows a completed exercise; the second figure was produced by rotating the first figure one position (one quarter-turn) counterclockwise. What relationship are you to show in D-36?
Answer: Reflect about the vertical. Ask a student to draw the figure on the transparency.

Discuss the illustration, pointing out the position of the various parts of the figure.

Remove the transparency and project **D-51** from the transparency of page 245.

These exercises are similar, but here you are not given a stated relationship. You are to examine figures A and B, determine the relationship between them, and draw a figure that has this same relationship to figure C. In exercise D-51, how do the circles in positions A and B differ?

Answer: Circle **B** is smaller and rotated one quarter-turn counterclockwise.

What should be drawn in position D to show the same relationship to figure C?

Answer: A smaller square divided into four equal squares with the lower left corner shaded in.

A figural analogy may have more than one correct interpretation. Does anyone see another possible solution to exercise D-51?

Answer: Reduce size and reflect about the vertical.

How would you draw figure D to show this relationship?

Answer: A smaller square divided into four equal squares with the top right corner shaded in.

Decrease size and: *or*

rotate one   reflect about
position counterclockwise   the vertical

GUIDED PRACTICE:

EXERCISES: **D-37, D-38, D-52, D-53**

Give students sufficient time to complete these exercises. Then, using the demonstration methodology above, have them discuss and explain their choices.

ANSWERS:

D-37   **D-38**   **D-52**   **D-53**

    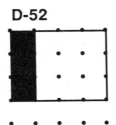 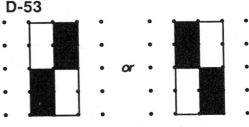

Rotate one position
clockwise and color
opposite.

Rotate one position and
add detail.

INDEPENDENT PRACTICE:

Assign exercises **D-39** through **D-50** and **D-54** through **D-65**

DISCUSSION TIPS:

Encourage students to describe the markings and relationships using the terms learned in the **FIGURAL SEQUENCES** section, e.g., **opposite**, **reflection**, **rotation**, **clockwise**, and **counterclockwise**.

ANSWERS:
NOTE: Alternate answers may be possible.

D-39

D-40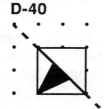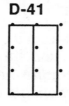

D-41

D-42 ...

D-39

D-40

D-41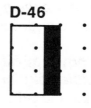

D-42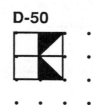

D-43

D-44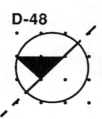

D-45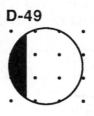

D-46 ...

D-47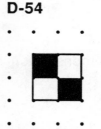

D-48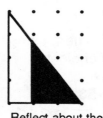

D-49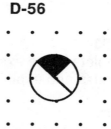

D-50

D-54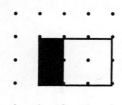

Make the figure uniform in two directions and add detail.

D-55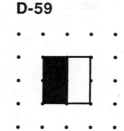

Reflect about the vertical.

D-56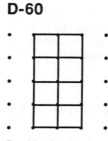

Reflect about the \ diagonal and reduce size.

D-57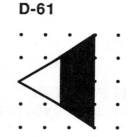

Reflect about the horizontal and increase size.

D-58

Rotate one position clockwise and color opposite.

D-59

Reflect about the vertical and reduce size.

D-60

Double the number of parts vertically.

D-61

Reflect about the vertical and color opposite.

D-62

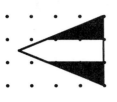

Rotate one-quarter
turn and color
opposite.

D-63

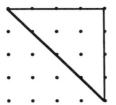

Rotate one-quarter
turn clockwise and
increase size.

D-64

Make an equilateral
shape, decreasing
the number of sides
by one.

D-65

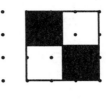

Rotate one-quarter
turn and shade
opposite section.

FOLLOW-UP REFERENT:

When might you need to supply a pair or a set that has the same relationship as another pair or set?

Examples: repeating weaving or needlework patterns in different colors; matching clothing or linens; selecting proper hardware for construction projects; wood, metal, or leather working projects

CURRICULUM APPLICATION:

Language Arts: recognizing correct pronunciation of words by comparing letter patterns

Mathematics: geometry exercises involving similarity, congruence, rotation, or reflection; recognizing equivalent fractional parts; working with ratios; writing and recognizing arithmetic problems in pictorial form

Science: seeing and stating relationships between different natural phenomena, animal or plant classes, or minerals and rocks; naming analogous body parts of different organisms; comparing and/or contrasting organisms or tissue types

Social Studies: recognizing and stating the relationship between people and events; recognizing and stating causal relationships

Enrichment Areas: learning vocabulary in a foreign language; recognizing types of music by listening to the rhythm, e.g., march, rumba, waltz; scale drawings

EXTENDING ACTIVITIES:

Figural Analogies, Book C-1, pp. 4–7

FIGURAL ANALOGIES—FOLLOW THE RULE

STRAND: Figural Analogies   **PAGES:** 248–249

ADDITIONAL MATERIALS:

Transparency of student workbook page 248
Washable transparency marker

INTRODUCTION:

In the previous exercise you produced a figure to complete an analogy.

OBJECTIVE:

In these exercises you will complete analogies by producing two figures which follow the given rule.

DEMONSTRATION/EXPLANATION:

Project exercise **D-66** from the transparency of page 248.

Read the rule and look at the first figure.

Pause.

Following the rule, what figure would you draw on the first grid?

Answer: A smaller circle with the colors reversed. Have a student draw the figure on the transparency, then confirm the answer by having the class compare the drawing to the rule.

Is the second circle smaller than the first?

Pause for confirmation.

Are the figures colored opposite?

Pause for confirmation.

Now look at the square in position C. Who would like to draw a figure to complete this analogy?

Pause for student demonstration, then confirm the answer by comparing it to the rule.

Answer:

GUIDED PRACTICE:

EXERCISE: **D-67**

Give students sufficient time to complete this exercise. Then, using the demonstration methodology above, have them discuss and explain their drawings.

ANSWER:

D-67

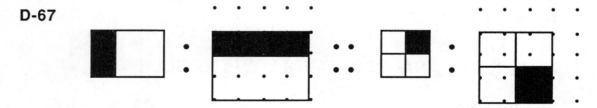

INDEPENDENT PRACTICE:

Assign exercises **D-68** through **D-73**

DISCUSSION TIPS:

Some exercises may have multiple interpretations. Encourage students to illustrate and explain any alternate solutions.

ANSWERS:

D-68

D-69

D-70

D-71

D-72

D-73

FOLLOW-UP REFERENT:

When might you use the ability to draw or supply something to illustrate a given relationship?

Examples: repeating weaving or needlework patterns in different colors; matching clothing, accessories, or linens; test-taking skills; arranging containers or dishes on shelves; selecting related containers, tools, or fasteners, e.g., nuts, bolts, screws; drawing or changing geometric shapes according to instructions; making directed changes in blueprints, drafting projects, or patterns

CURRICULUM APPLICATION:

Language Arts: changing formats of letters, outlines, or compositions

Mathematics: comparing angles or polygons; recognizing and illustrating changes in formats of mathematical problems

Science: observing and describing analogous structures in plants and animals; observing and describing changes in weather patterns, cloud formations, etc.

Social Studies: changing charts or graphs to reflect changed information

Enrichment Areas: changing parts of art, home economics, or industrial arts projects according to instructions; making or recognizing changes in pattern plays in sports or individual steps in a dance routine

EXTENDING ACTIVITIES:

None.

FIGURAL ANALOGIES—SUPPLY A PAIR

STRAND: Figural Analogies   **PAGES:** 250–251

ADDITIONAL MATERIALS:

Transparency of student workbook page 250
Washable transparency marker

INTRODUCTION:

In the previous exercise you produced figures to show a specific relationship.

OBJECTIVE:

In these exercises you will determine the relationship illustrated by the first part of an analogy and draw a pair of figures which completes the analogy.

DEMONSTRATION/EXPLANATION:

Project the transparency of page 250.

In exercise D-74, how would you change figure A to produce figure B?

Answer: Rotate the circle one quarter-turn counterclockwise and color opposite.

Who would like to draw two figures on the grid to complete this analogy?

Pause for student demonstration, then confirm that the drawings reflect the correct relationship. Sample answer:

Are these the only two figures which will complete the analogy correctly?

Answer: No; any two figures which show the same relationship can be used.

Now look at exercise D-75. How is figure A changed to produce figure B?

Answer: The square is reflected about the northeast/southwest diagonal and some detail has been subtracted.

Who would like to draw two figures that will complete this analogy?

Pause for student demonstration, then confirm drawings and erase the transparency.
Sample answer:

Can someone supply a different pair of figures?

Pause for a second demonstration, then confirm answers by stating the relationship and comparing the answers.

GUIDED PRACTICE:
EXERCISES: **D-76, D-77**
Give students sufficient time to complete these exercises. Then, using the demonstration methodology above, have them discuss and explain their choices.
ANSWERS:

D-76

Reflect about the vertical, color opposite, and reduce size.

D-77

Reflect about the horizontal and color opposite.

INDEPENDENT PRACTICE:
Assign exercises **D-78** through **D-81**

DISCUSSION TIPS:
Encourage students to use the terms learned in the previous lesson when describing the markings and relationships.

ANSWERS:
D-78

Rotate one quarter-turn counterclockwise, increase size, and color opposite.

D-79

Reflect about the \ diagonal and increase size.

D-80

Rotate one quarter-turn clockwise, reduce size, and color opposite.

D-81

Reflect about the / diagonal and reduce size.

FOLLOW-UP REFERENT:
When might you use the ability to supply a pair or set with the same relationship as another pair or set?

Examples: repeating weaving or needlework patterns in different colors; matching clothing, accessories, or linens; test-taking skills; arranging containers or dishes on shelves; selecting related containers, tools, or fasteners, e.g., nuts, bolts, screws; drawing or changing geometric shapes according to instructions; making directed changes in blueprints, drafting projects, or patterns

CURRICULUM APPLICATION:
Language Arts: changing formats of letters, outlines, or compositions
Mathematics: comparing angles or polygons; recognizing and illustrating changes in
  formats of mathematical problems
Science: observing and describing analogous structures in plants and animals;
  observing and describing changes in weather patterns, cloud formations, etc.
Social Studies: changing charts or graphs to reflect changed information
Enrichment Areas: changing parts of art, home economics, or industrial arts projects
  according to instructions; making or recognizing changes in pattern plays in sports or
  in individual steps in a dance routine

EXTENDING ACTIVITIES:
None.

FIGURAL ANALOGIES—SELECT THE SOLID

STRAND: Figural Analogies   **PAGES:** 252–257

ADDITIONAL MATERIALS:
Transparency of student workbook page 252
Washable transparency marker

INTRODUCTION:
In previous exercises you selected or drew figures to complete analogies.

OBJECTIVE:
In these exercises you will select a solid which correctly completes an analogy.

DEMONSTRATION/EXPLANATION:
Project the **EXAMPLE** from the transparency of page 252.
Here are two views of the same solid. How was the second view produced from the first view?
Answer: The solid was rotated.
How did the position of the face marked with an X change?
Answer: It moved from the right face to the front face.
Which direction did the solid turn?
Answer: To the left.
If the L-shaped solid in the third position is also turned to the left, how will it look?
Answer: The face on the right (steps) will turn to the front.
Which figure correctly completes the analogy?
Answer: **c**

GUIDED PRACTICE:
EXERCISES: **D-82, D-83**

Give students sufficient time to complete these exercises. Then, using the demonstration methodology above, have them discuss and explain their choices.
ANSWERS: **D-82** b (add detail, doubling the number of parts <u>or</u> adding one part);
D-83 b (subtract detail, halving the number of parts)

INDEPENDENT PRACTICE:
Assign exercises **D-84** through **D-104**

DISCUSSION TIPS:
Encourage students to describe figures using terms they learned in the **FIGURAL SEQUENCES** section, e.g., **rotating, tumbling, left, right, counterclockwise,** and **clockwise**. Rotations of solids are illustrated below:

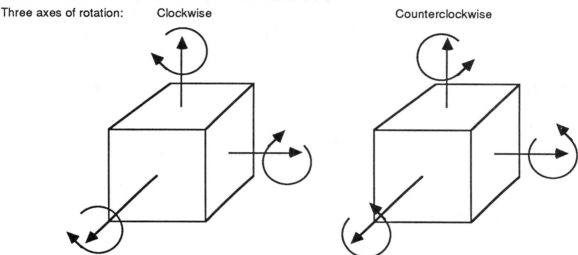

Three axes of rotation: Clockwise   Counterclockwise

ANSWERS:
D-84 b (rotate clockwise about the vertical axis and reduce size); **D-85** b (rotate forward about the left-right horizontal axis and increase size); **D-86** c (rotate backward about the left-right horizontal axis and reduce size)

D-87 d (rotate counterclockwise about the front-back horizontal axis); **D-88** c (rotate counterclockwise about the vertical axis); **D-89** f (rotate forward about the left-right horizontal axis); **D-90** a (rotate clockwise about the vertical axis)

D-91 b (rotate backward about the left-right horizontal axis); **D-92** e (rotate clockwise about the front-back horizontal axis); **D-93** g (rotate clockwise about the vertical axis); **D-94** c (rotate forward about the left-right horizontal axis); **D-95** d (rotate counterclockwise about the front-back horizontal axis)

D-96 e (rotate about the front-back horizontal axis in either direction); **D-97** c (rotate about the vertical axis); **D-98** b (rotate about the left-right horizontal axis in either direction); **D-99** d (rotate about the vertical in either direction)

D-100 c (rotate clockwise about the vertical axis); **D-101** f (rotate backward about the left-right horizontal axis); **D-102** a (rotate counterclockwise about the vertical axis); **D-103** e (rotate forward about the left-right horizontal axis); **D-104** d (rotate clockwise about the front-back horizontal axis)

FOLLOW-UP REFERENT:
When might you need to recognize changes in a solid?
Examples: model building; assembling cardboard file boxes or airline boxes for soft luggage; assembling display racks; games involving dice or construction

CURRICULUM APPLICATION:
Language Arts: ——————
Mathematics: position discrimination involving cubes and prisms; geometry exercises involving rotation of solids
Science: observing different views of organisms or geological features
Social Studies: ——————
Enrichment Areas: test-taking skills; career education discussions involving architects, engineers, electricians, construction tradesmen, draftsmen, graphic designers, dentists, radiologists, and field archaeologists; design principles in sculpture and making molds; drafting and architectural drawing; reading blueprints; industrial arts projects

EXTENDING ACTIVITIES:
None.

FIGURAL ANALOGIES—SELECT THE CUBE

STRAND: Figural Analogies   **PAGES:** 258–259

ADDITIONAL MATERIALS:
Transparencies of student workbook pages 183, 184, and 258
Washable transparency marker

INTRODUCTION:
In the previous exercise you selected a solid to complete an analogy.

OBJECTIVE:
In these exercises you will select a cube to complete an analogy involving rotation.

DEMONSTRATION/EXPLANATION:
Project the transparency of page 183.
Remember how the left or right face changes when a solid rotates about the vertical axis? If it rotates to the right, the number that was on the front moves to the right face. If it rotates to the left, the front face becomes the left face. The numeral on the top face remains the same numeral, but changes position.
Project the top section from the transparency of page 184.
Either the top or bottom face becomes the front face if the solid rotates about the left-right horizontal axis. The numeral on the right face changes position.
Project the bottom section from the transparency of page 184.
If a solid rotates about the front-back horizontal axis, either the left or right face becomes the top face, and the numeral on the front changes position.
Project the **EXAMPLE** from the transparency of page 258.

In this EXAMPLE, A and B are two views of the cube shown at the top of the screen. How would you move the first view to produce the second view?

Answer: Rotate the cube counterclockwise about the front-back horizontal (tumble it to the left).

You can tell the cube is rotating to the left because the right face becomes the top. Which view in the CHOICE BOX represents how cube C will look after it has been moved in the same manner?

Ask students to explain how they arrived at their answers. Answer: **b**; the **2** on the right face is now on top and the **5** on the front face has rotated counterclockwise.

GUIDED PRACTICE:
EXERCISES: **D-105, D-106**

Give students sufficient time to complete these exercises. Then, using the demonstration methodology above, have them discuss and explain their choices.

ANSWERS: **D-105** d (rotate forward about the left-right horizontal); **D-106** e (rotate counterclockwise about the vertical)

INDEPENDENT PRACTICE:
Assign exercises **D-107** through **D-111**

DISCUSSION TIPS:
Encourage students to describe the markings and relationships using the terms learned in the **FIGURAL SEQUENCES** section, e.g., **rotating, tumbling, left, right, clockwise,** and **counterclockwise.**

ANSWERS:
D-107 c (rotate clockwise about the front-back horizontal); **D-108** d (rotate clockwise about the vertical); **D-109** a (rotate backward about the left-right horizontal); **D-110** e (rotate clockwise about the front-back horizontal); **D-111** c (rotate counterclockwise about the vertical)

FOLLOW-UP REFERENT:
When might you need to recognize the relative position of the sides of a cube?

Examples: model building; assembling cardboard file boxes or airline boxes for soft luggage; assembling display racks; games involving dice or construction

CURRICULUM APPLICATION:
Language Arts: —————

Mathematics: position discrimination involving cubes and prisms; geometry exercises involving the rotation of solids

Science: observing different views of organisms or geological features

Social Studies: —————

Enrichment Areas: test-taking skills; career education discussions involving architects, engineers, electricians, construction tradesmen, draftsmen, graphic designers, dentists, radiologists, field archaeologists; design principles in sculpture; making molds; drafting and architectural drawing; reading blueprints; industrial arts projects

EXTENDING ACTIVITIES:
None.

TRANSPARENCY MASTERS

FOR

BUILDING THINKING SKILLS LESSON PLANS

TM # refers to **Transparency Master Number**. These are referenced by number under **ADDITIONAL MATERIALS** in the individual Lesson Plans to which they apply.

HEADINGS match the bold type lesson titles at the top of the corresponding page in the student workbook and the individual Lesson Plan to which each TM applies. The page number included in the headings refer to student workbook pages.

INSTRUCTIONS to the teacher appear in parentheses; instructions to students appear in **bold type**. Dotted lines indicate figures which are to be cut out of the transparency so they can be moved around.

Please note that it is possible to make these transparencies of the TM pages <u>and</u> the student workbook pages on an ordinary copier. See specific instructions for your copy machine or check with a firm which supplies transparency masters for directions. It is <u>not</u> necessary to remove the TM pages from this book to make transparencies in this manner.

TRANSPARENCY MASTER (TM) #1

MATCHING FIGURES, student workbook, p. 1

Figure a

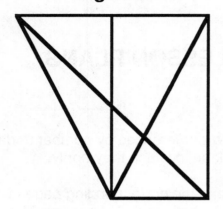

Figure b

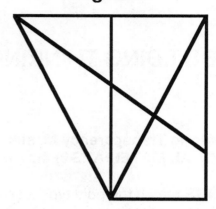

Figure c

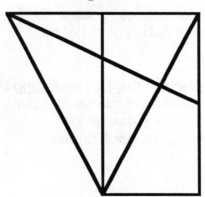

Figure d

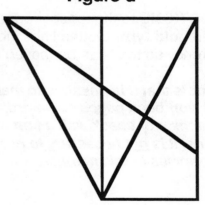

(Cut out movable figures below.)

1

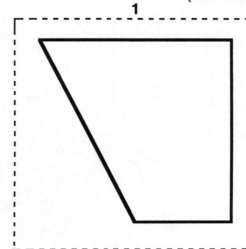

2

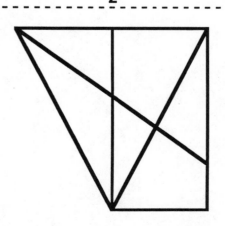

TM #2

WHICH FIGURE DOES NOT MATCH?, p. 3

Figure a

Figure b

Figure c

Figure d

(Movable figure–cut out)

TM #3

FINDING SHAPES, p. 11

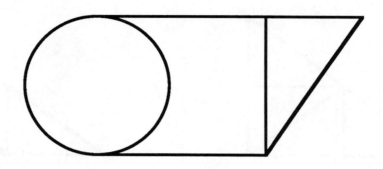

(Cut out pattern pieces below.)

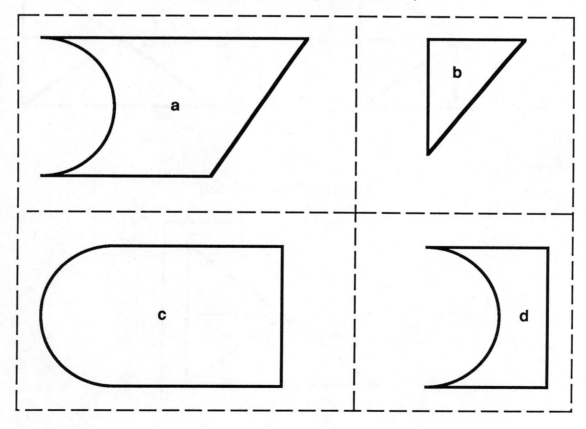

TM #4

COMBINING SHAPES, p. 14

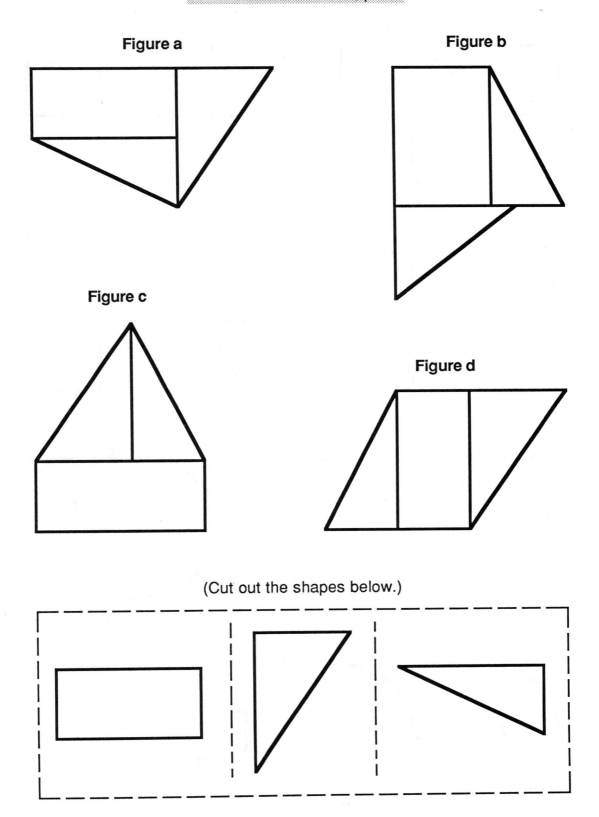

Figure a

Figure b

Figure c

Figure d

(Cut out the shapes below.)

TM #5

RECOMBINING SHAPES, p. 18

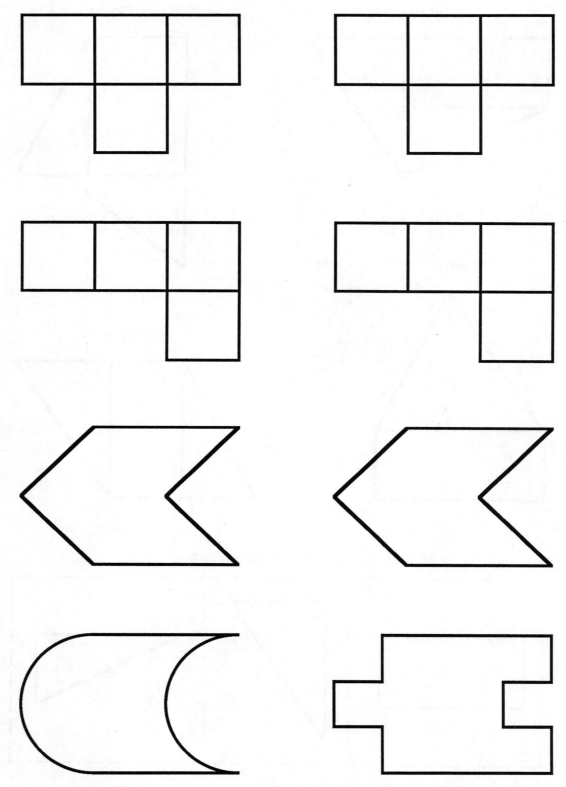

TM #6

WHAT SHAPE COMPLETES THE SQUARE? p. 20

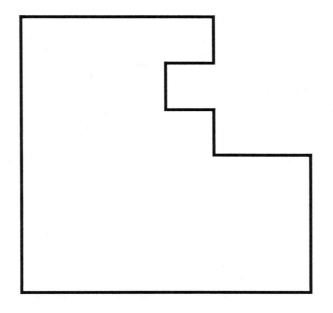

(Cut out movable shapes below.)

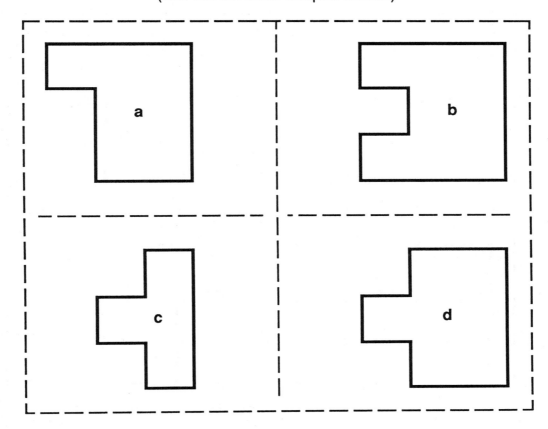

TM #7

COMPLETING THE SQUARE WITH TWO SHAPES, p. 22

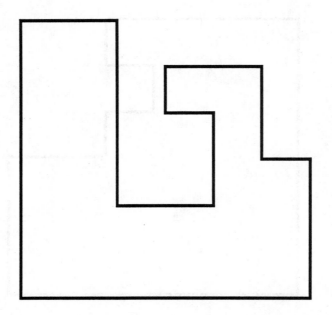

(Cut out movable shapes below.)

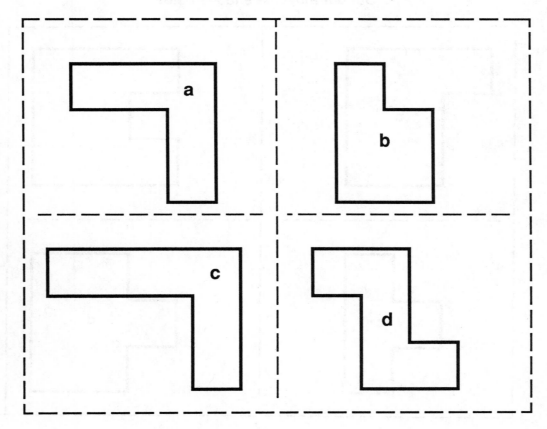

TM #8

MATCHING CONGRUENT SHAPES, p. 24

(Cut out lettered shapes)

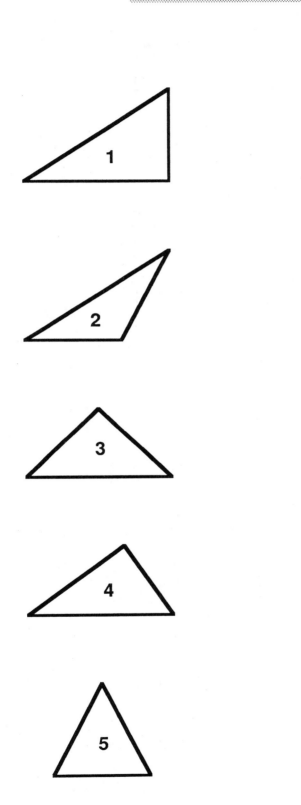

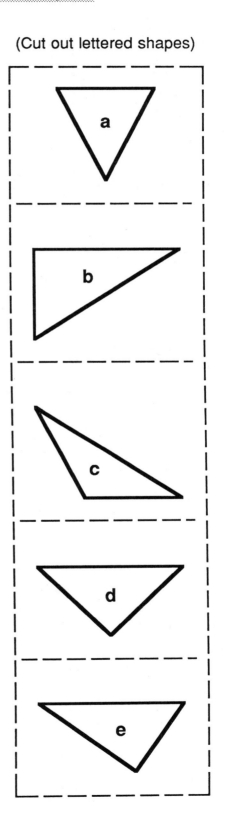

TM #9

RECOGNIZING CONGRUENT PARTS, p. 28

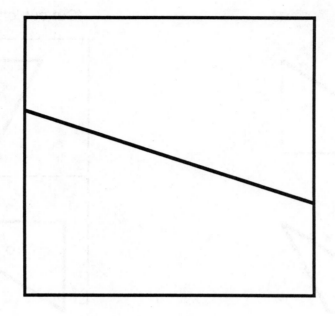

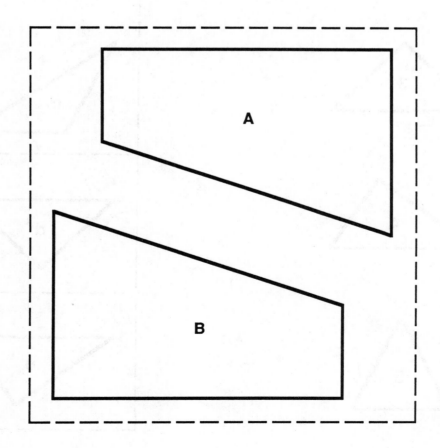

TM #10

DIVIDING SHAPES INTO CONGRUENT PARTS, p. 32

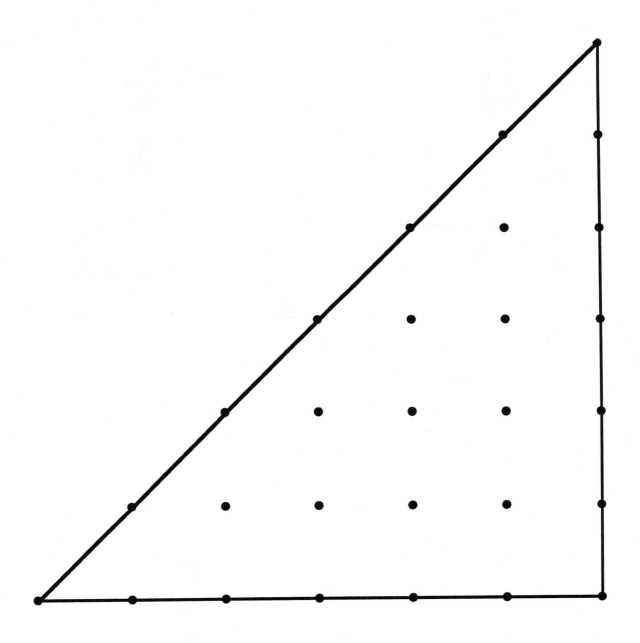

TM #11

RECOGNIZING LINES OF SYMMETRY, p. 60

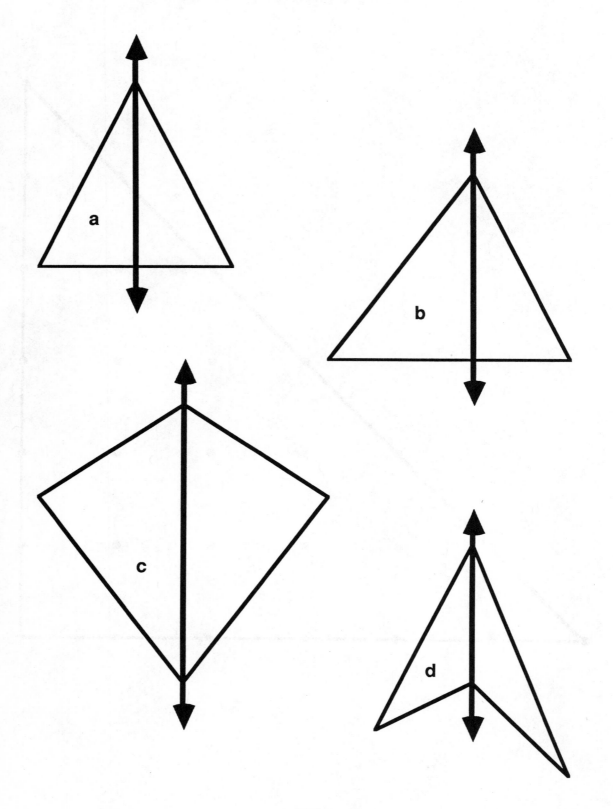

TM #12

DRAWING LINES OF SYMMETRY, p. 62

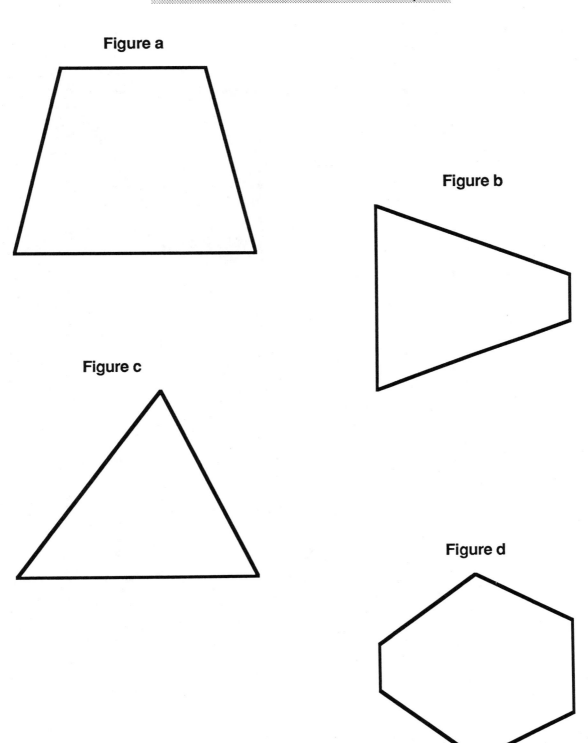

Figure a

Figure b

Figure c

Figure d

TM #13

PRODUCING SYMMETRICAL SHAPES, p. 64

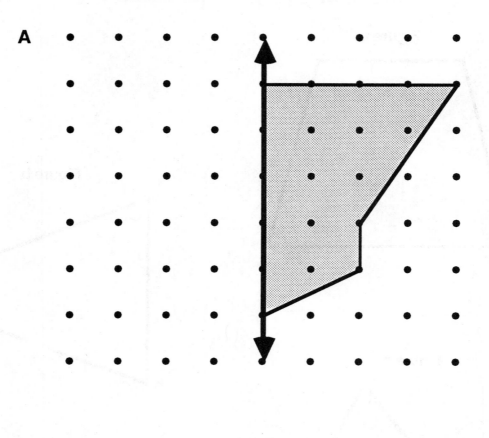

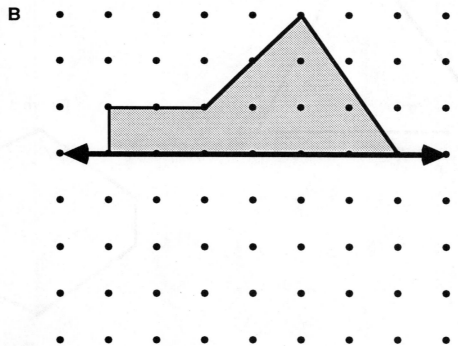

TM #14

DRAWING MULTIPLE LINES OF SYMMETRY, p. 66

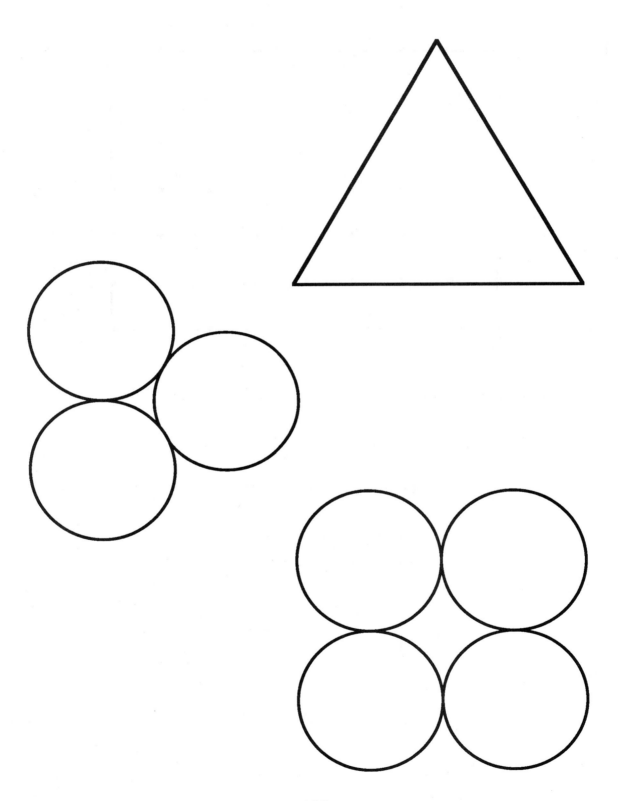

TM #15

COVERING A SURFACE, p. 68

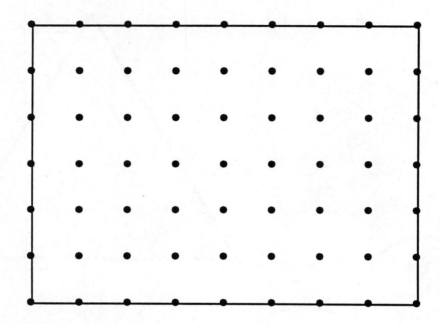

(Cut out the shape below to use as a pattern.)

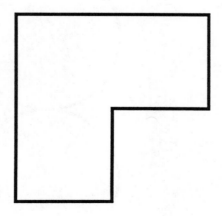

TM #16

(Cut out each shape below.)

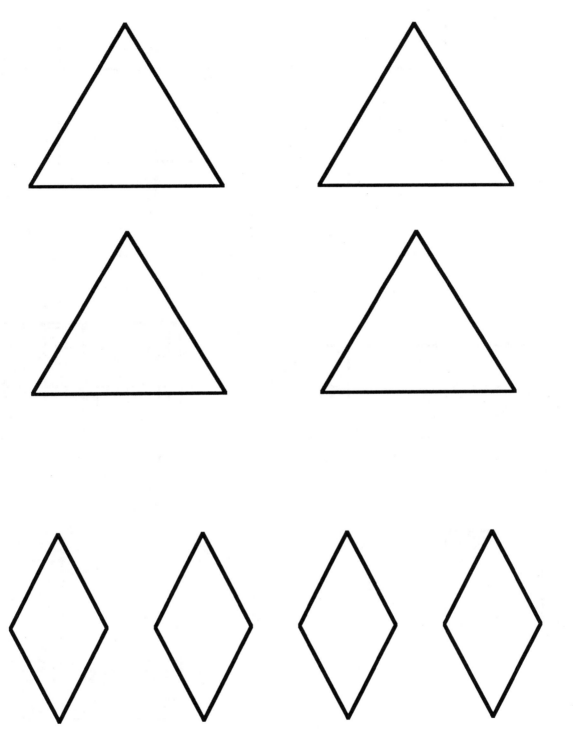

TM #17

POLYOMINOES, p. 76

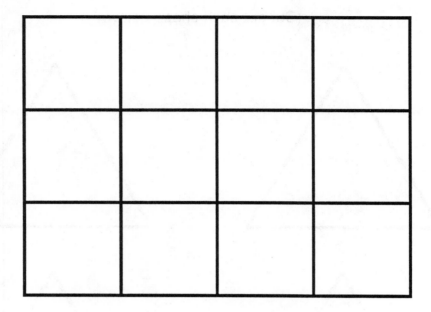

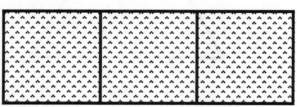

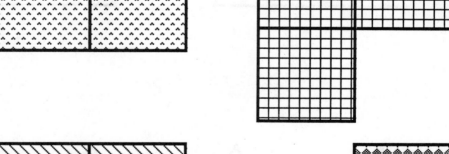

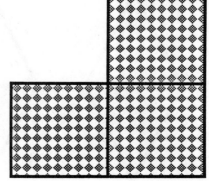

TM #18

SEQUENCE OF FIGURES—SELECT, p. 103

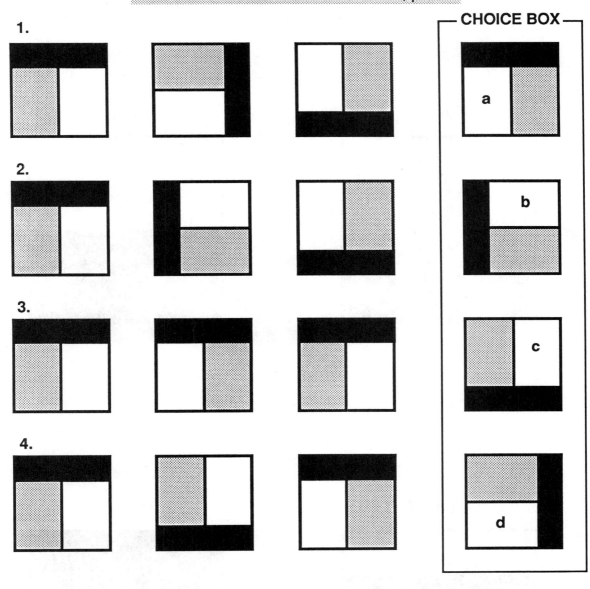

(Cut out the enlarged figure to the right
and use to demonstrate
rotations and reflections.)

197

TM #19

SEQUENCE OF FIGURES—SELECT, p. 103

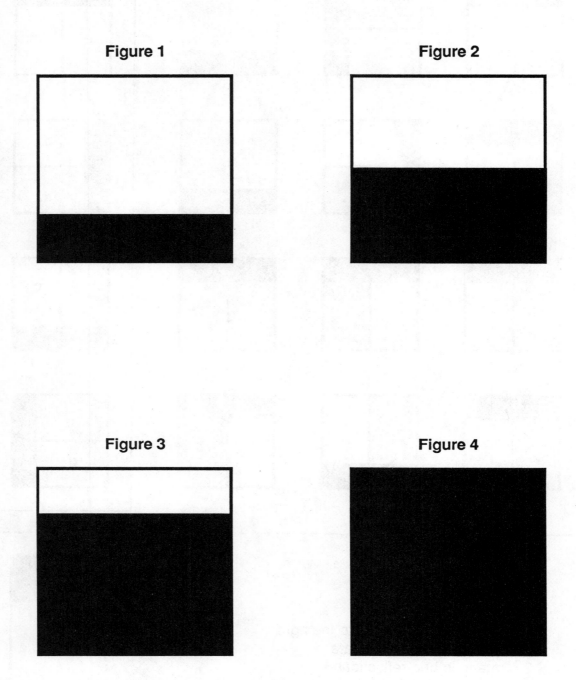

Figure 1

Figure 2

Figure 3

Figure 4

TM #20

SEQUENCE OF FIGURES—SUPPLY, p. 109

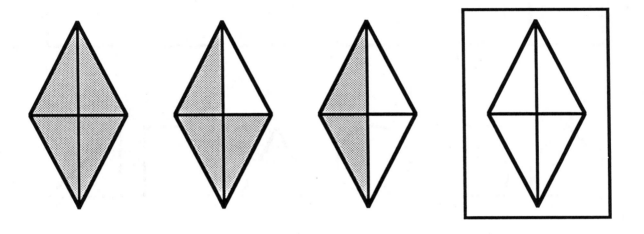

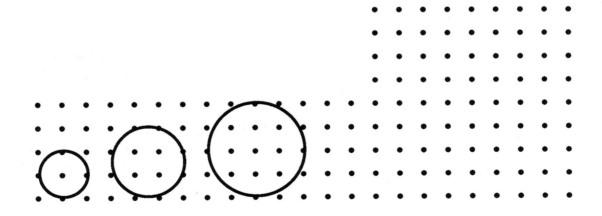

TM #21

SEQUENCE OF SHAPES—SUPPLY, p. 110

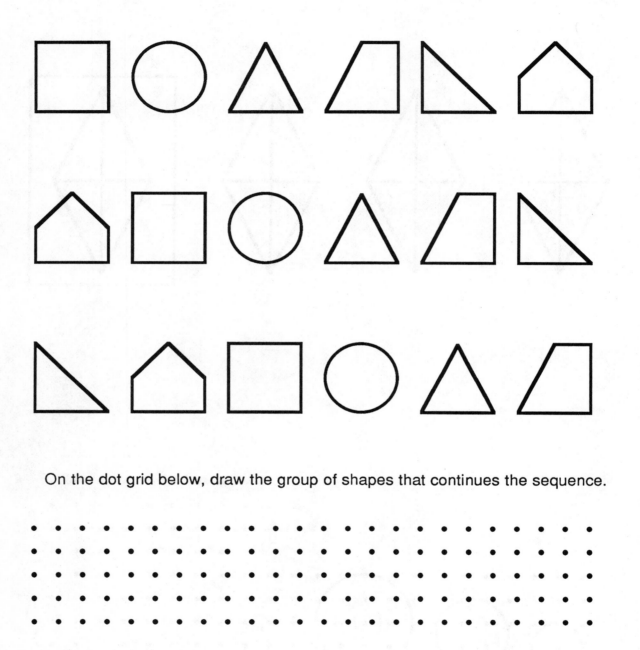

On the dot grid below, draw the group of shapes that continues the sequence.

TM #22

ROTATING FIGURES—FIND THE EXCEPTION, p. 113

(Cut out all the pieces.)

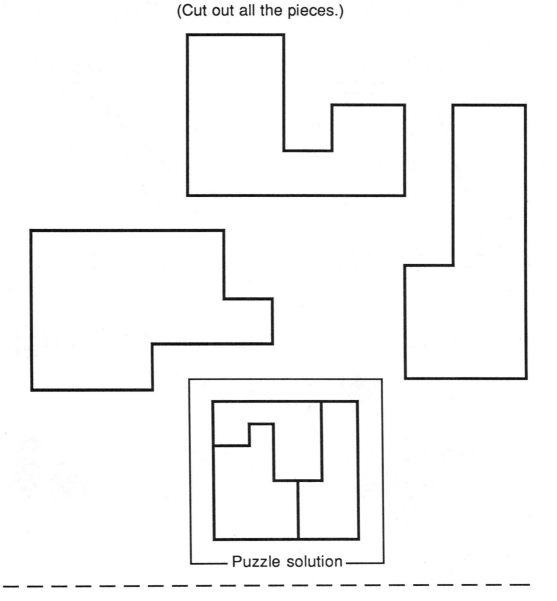

─ Puzzle solution ─

- -

Figure A

Figure B

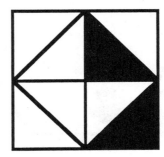

TM #23

ROTATING FIGURES—SUPPLY, pp. 115–119

(Cut out all the pieces and use to illustrate exercises.)

(EXAMPLE, P. 115)

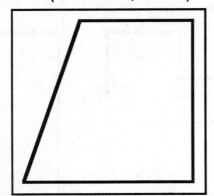

(B-50, p. 115)

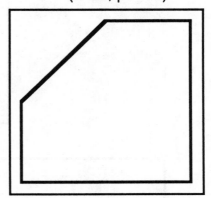

(B-57, p. 117)

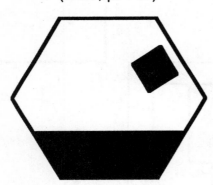

(EXAMPLE, p. 118)

(B-62, p. 118)

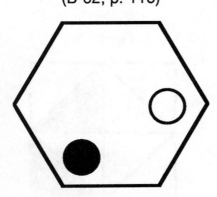

(B-65, p. 119)

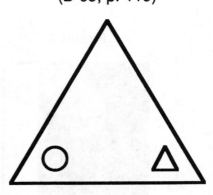

TM #24

(Cut out all the pieces and use to illustrate exercises.)

A
(EXAMPLE, p. 120, B-89, B-94)

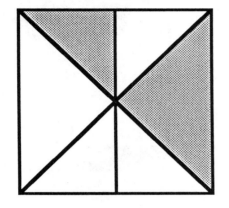

B
(EXAMPLE, p. 121)

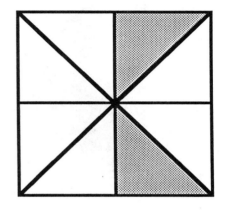

(B-78, B-82, B-88, B-92)

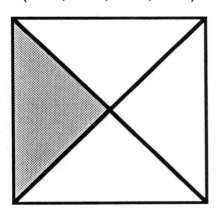

(B-71, B-73, B-79, B-81)

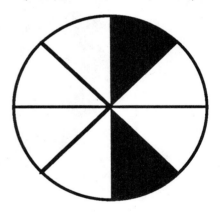

(B-84, B-85)

(B-86)

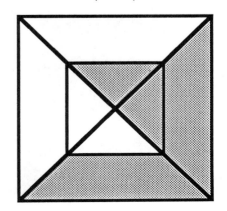

TM #25

MULTIPLE REFLECTIONS, pp. 122-127

(Cut out all the pieces and use to illustrate exercises.)

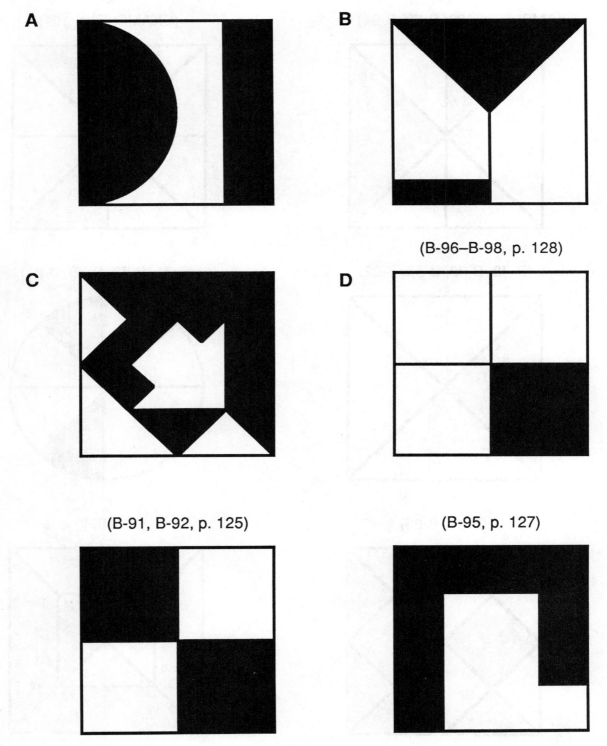

A

B

(B-96–B-98, p. 128)

C

D

(B-91, B-92, p. 125)

(B-95, p. 127)

TM #26

EXPLAINING ROTATION OR REFLECTION, p. 130

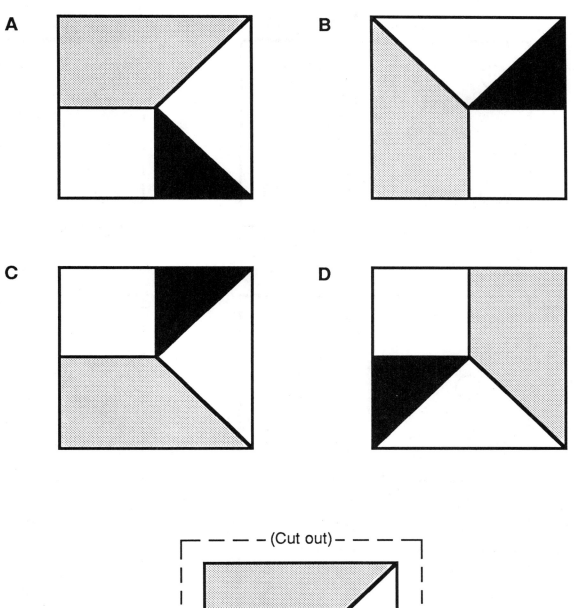

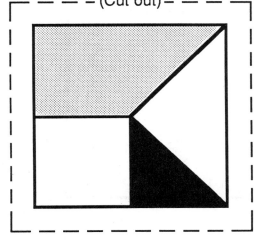

205

TM #27

PAPER FOLDING—SELECT, p. 132

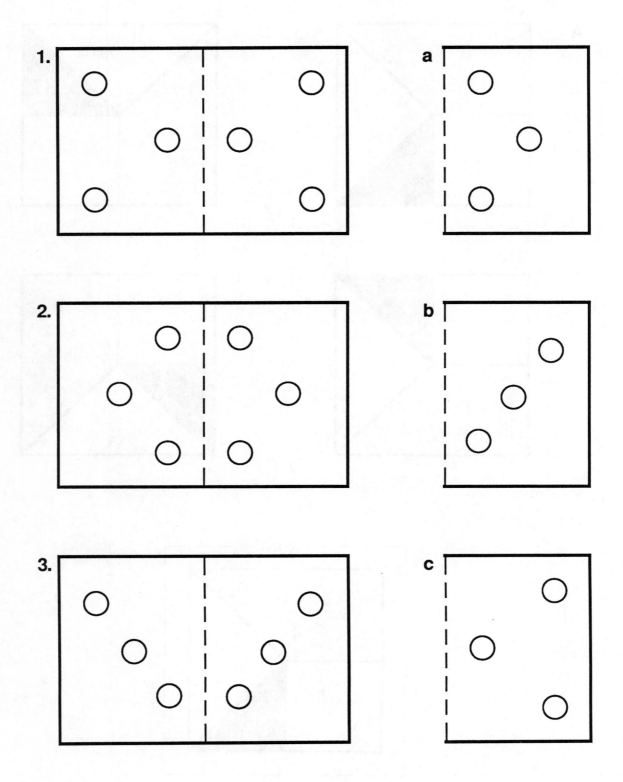

TM #28

FIGURAL ANALOGIES—SELECT, p. 233

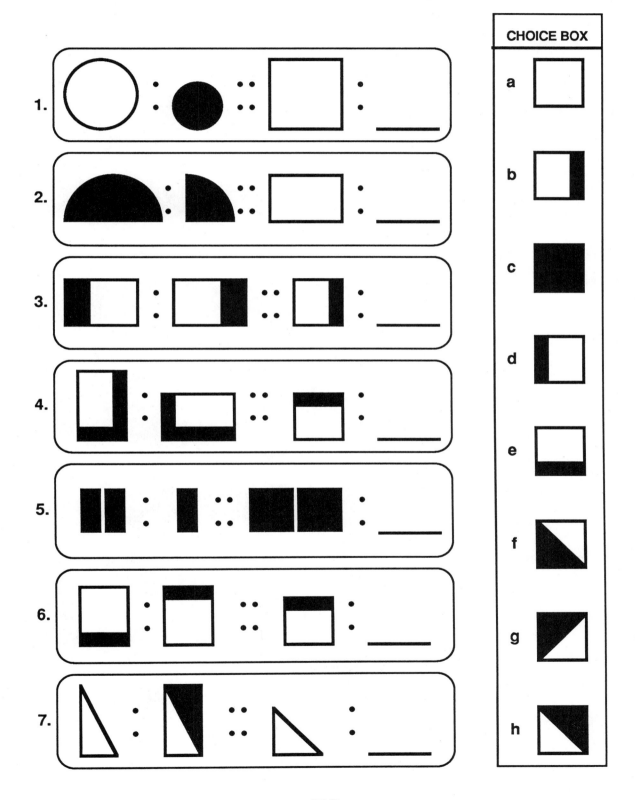